Introduction

Let's start with a challenge.

You are a Product Manager, Product Leader or Founder (hopefully you are, if you are reading this book).

Imagine I ask you to do the following:

Build a product to out-compete Gmail.

Yes, that Gmail.

The one with 1.5 billion active users, generating billions of dollars in revenue...

Understandably, you might say:

"Impossible! It can't be done."

An experienced product leader might even explain WHY it can't be done, talking about the power of network effects, of Google's market dominance, of superior engineering, etc.

Yet one small startup, founded in 2015, has not only out-competed Gmail, but has a waiting list of 750k potential users.

They even charge each user $30/month to use their product (5x what Gmail charges).

How?

It all comes down to one thing:

Product strategy.

Specifically, knowing:

1. How to **define** the right product strategy to gain initial success
2. How to **communicate** that product strategy so people actually follow it
3. How to **remain relentlessly focused** on executing that product strategy to maintain success

(But more on the story behind that startup in Chapter 2, when we cover how to uncover the right product strategy.)

Product success or failure depends *primarily* on one key thing:

Product strategy.

Without a product strategy, no product can sustain success in the long-term.

This book has been written to help you master product strategy.

In the next chapter, using data & real-world examples, I will break down why product strategy is crucial success & why most companies either do not have a product strategy (or have the wrong product strategy.)

In the following chapters, I will then breakdown how to actually craft & communicate your own product strategy into simple steps for you to put into practice with your own product or products.

Specifically, I will teach you to:

1. Understand what product strategy is & demonstrate (using data) why it is essential to product success
2. Define the right problems & niches to focus on
3. Uncover unique value in your product's market
4. Understand & apply long-term strategies for success
5. Craft & validate your product strategy before building a thing
6. Communicate your product strategy effectively to stakeholders

And, most importantly, teach this in as *simple & actionable* a way possible so that you actually go and put this stuff into practice!

Because if you want to just flick through this book out of curiosity, put it down now.

It will be a waste of your time & a waste of my time writing this book!

True learning - true experience - only comes from putting theory into practice. From learning, then applying.

And we've made applying the theory super simple, with [ready-made Miro templates](https://miro.com/miroverse/profile/prod-mba/) you can download & start working on at the end of each chapter.

(If you're reading a physical copy, you can find that Miro template at https://miro.com/miroverse/profile/prod-mba/ - download the board called "Product Thinking Board").

So, before getting started, ask yourself:

Are you serious about mastering product strategy? Are you serious about leveling-up your product career?

If so, turn to the next page.

Let's jump in.

What is Product Strategy?

Before we get ahead of ourselves, it's worth starting with a simple, yet commonly misunderstood, question:

What is a product?

A product is essentially a vehicle for solving a problem for a specific group of people.

Its purpose is:

1. To *create* value for that specific group with a product they love
2. To *capture* some of that value for the business that created it (in the form of revenue)

Obvious, right?

What is not usually obvious, however, is that "the product" does not just consist of some sort of core technology, or "the app" part of your user's experience.

The product should be understood more holistically to include:

1. How we **acquire** our users

2. How we **activate** those users (for example, getting their first bit of key value from us)
3. How we **retain** those users
4. How we generate **revenue** from those users
5. How we can drive **referral** from those users

Why?

Because all the different building blocks of a product ultimately contribute towards the same promise we make - as well as what we ultimately deliver - to our users and/or customers.

If we promise one thing, but deliver another thing, then we will fail to attract the right users & will struggle to get them to use our product - let alone retain them, charge them for the product or get them to refer others to the product.

Seen through such a lens, all teams within our organisation - however those teams may be structured - should be driving towards the same set of objectives.

We do not, for example, have sales doing one thing, marketing another, and our tech team working on something completely unrelated.

All teams do product work.

All teams contribute towards the success of our product.

And product strategy is the thing that ties all of this work together.

What is strategy?

Furthermore, we must be clear about what exactly we mean when we use the word "strategy" before talking specifically about "product strategy".

Strategy is commonly understood to be some sort of plan (a list of things to work on), or a goal (such as "to dominate the headphones market").

However, strategy is neither a plan nor a goal.

In his book, *Good Strategy Bad Strategy: The Difference and Why It Matters*, author Richard Rumelt draws an important distinction between goal setting and strategy,

> "Unlike a stand- alone decision or a goal, a strategy is a coherent set of analyses, concepts, policies, arguments, and actions that respond to a high-stakes challenge."

With this definition, let's compare a plan v. A goal v. A strategy:

Plan: *"Let's build everything our customers request"* would be an example of a plan, as we would be building a generic to-do list.

Goal: *"Let's be the best email app in the world"* would be an example of a goal, because it just outlines a desired business outcome (not how to achieve that outcome).

Strategy: *"Let's focus on providing world-class customer service in order to provide a better service than the competition"* would be an example of a strategy because:

1. It represents an analysis (we can assume that a focus on "world-class customer service" has been chosen for a reason, such as a way to differentiate our product)
2. It provides an argument underpinning how we will drive towards a "high-stakes" goal (in this case, beating the competition)

Personally, I prefer a more simple way of understanding strategy. From Michael Porterer:

> "The essence of strategy is choosing what *not* to do"

Strategy helps us determine what we should work on, in which order we should work on those things - and it should make clear what we should NOT work on.

Using our example above as an example, that would mean we focus on "world-class customer service" and don't worry about everything else we *could* do to provide value with our product.

What is a product strategy?

We now understand what a product is: A vehicle for delivering value for our target market & for us as a business.

We also know what strategy is: A framework for determining what we do - and do not - focus on in order to achieve a goal.

What, therefore, is a product strategy?

On a basic level, product strategy is what we use to determine what we should - and should not focus on - in order for our product to be successful (i.e. to deliver enough value to our users that they sign up & use our product, as well as enough value for our business that we can charge enough to make a profit).

Product Strategy

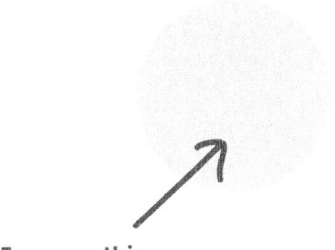

Focus on this...   **... NOT on these other things**

Example:

My company, Prod MBA, operates in a competitive market, with loads of books, videos, courses & consultants all vying to help Product Managers & leaders do their job better.

There are also many Venture Capital-backed businesses in our space, with literally 100x our budget.

Our core driver of success?

We focus exclusively on providing as "hands-on" & "actionable" a learning experience as possible.

We *promise* "hands-on, actionable" learning.

We *deliver* "hands-on, actionable" learning.

And we are successful because we *remain laser-focused* on promising & delivering even more "hands-on, actionable" learning with every iteration.

We don't, for example, try to have "the best known teachers" or "the best digital learning platform".

We don't think these are all that important, firstly.

Secondly, **they do not align with our product strategy.**

If something helps us be more "hands-on" and "actionable", we do it.

If not, it's just not relevant.

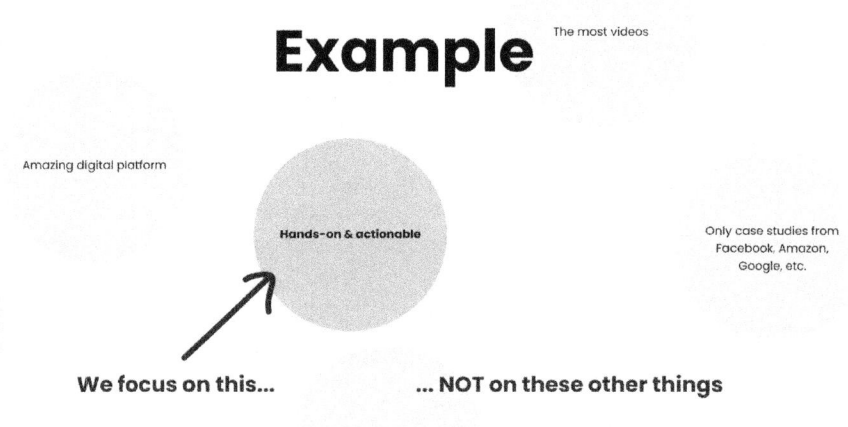

Sure, we are a small, bootstrapped company. Therefore we are forced by necessity to be extremely focused. However, the principle is true of ANY successful company:

No company can do everything.

Nor should it.

Comparing Product Strategy to Chess

The second key aspect of product strategy is about how we connect a series of actions to deliver long-term value.

Let's break down this definition by Melissa Perri, author of *Escaping The Build Trap*:

> "Product Strategy is a system of achievable goals and visions that work together to align the team around desirable outcomes for both the business and your customers."

The *"system of achievable goals and visions"* refers to the fact that most product strategies are sequential i.e. there are multiple steps to be achieved.

Think of a game of chess, but where we all start with a different set of pieces & those pieces can all move at once.

Some competitors might start with more knights, as they have more funding.

Others might start with more castles, as they have a better team (or certain specialists in their team).

But to play chess effectively, the pieces we start with on the board aren't the most important thing.

The most important thing? The order in which we make our moves.

In product strategy terms, the different pieces represent different teams. The different moves represent what those different teams work on.

We must make certain moves at certain moments for them to have impact, whilst also thinking about which moves our other pieces could make at that specific moment in time.

To use a real-world example, let's look at Tesla:

Tesla's product vision is to dominate the car market, bringing about an electric car revolution in the process.

Tesla's initial product strategy was to, in Elon Musk's words, *"enter at the high end of the market, where customers are prepared to pay a premium"*.

That wouldn't happen overnight, however.

Tesla therefore had to breakdown that product strategy - to work out a) which chess pieces they had & b) how they should play those pieces - in order to achieve that strategic goal.

That meant in practice:

1. Building an initial prototype with just a Lotus chassis with a prototype battery & engine
2. Then building & selling the Model S to a small group of early adopters in the US
3. Then iterating based on data & feedback they received
4. Then improving the Model S so the less forgiving general public saw it as a desirable, reliable car

Tesla's Strategic Steps

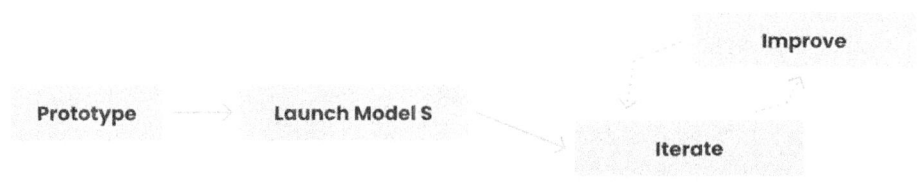

And, in fact, in Tesla's case, we see multiple product strategies tying together in order to drive towards that product vision:

1. Build sports car (Step 1, broken down above)
2. Use that money to build an affordable car
3. Use that money to build an even more affordable car
4. While doing above, also provide zero emission electric power generation options

So we see the two key elements of product strategy in practice:

1. A clear idea of what unique value we can offer (e.g. in Prod MBA's case, always being "hands-on" & "actionable", whilst ignoring everything else we could focus on.)

2. A clear idea of the possible chess moves we need to make in order to effectively deliver that unique value

Why do so many product teams not understand product strategy?

Finally, it's worth touching upon why product strategy is so misunderstood, despite the endless list of books, videos & courses on the subject.

From working with 30+ product teams & coaching over 290 Product Managers, I've observed that it comes down to this:

Over-complicating it.

They think that - in order to come up with a great product strategy - you need everything worked out from Day 1.

Take the following commonly accepted definition of product strategy:

> "The product strategy describes how the long-term goal is attained; it includes the product's value proposition, market, key features, and business goals."

— A definition of product strategy, *Strategize: Product Strategy and Product Roadmap Practices for the Digital Age*, Roman Pilcher

To have a product strategy, Pilcher implies we need to pretty much know exactly what we are building & have broken our product strategy down into concrete steps.

Sure, that's important. As illustrated by the Tesla example above, at some point we need to break down our product strategy into specific, sequential steps.

His definition is therefore not wrong.

But product strategy can be far more simple to start.

And such a complex definition prevents people - overwhelms them, even - from getting started with product strategy.

In reality, to get started, we don't need to define key features. Or a complex set of chess moves.

We only need a high-level idea of where to focus - and where not to focus.

And for you, starting out with product strategy, you just need to focus on answering the following question:

What truly unique value can your product provide?

Without being able to answer that question with a clear, credible answer, nothing else matters.

In the next chapter, I'll explain why being laser-focused on this question is becoming more & more important to product success as each year passes.

Why is Product Strategy So Important?

I came up with the idea for my first startup aged 20, travelling down the Brazilian Amazon by myself for 2 months.

"Wouldn't it be cool to plot my journey and connect with other travellers along on a beautiful, visual map?", I thought.

I called it BackTracker.

When I went back to the UK to finish my final year of university, I built a team, brought on some advisors and we got started building BackTracker.

In that first year, we made **every** mistake you could possibly think of:

From decisions driven by ego, not speaking to customers, to no thought to how to even make money!

The biggest mistake though?

A lack of product strategy.

Because we did, in fact, execute efficiently - and moved quickly.

We even got some traction, with 10k downloads in the first week of launching.

But we made one fatal mistake:

We tried to do everything.

Too many features.

Too many vague problems to solve.

Too broad a value proposition.

We simply had no focus.

Despite raising investment, going through an accelerator & being surrounded by a world-class mentorship team, after 2 years our mistakes caught up with us.

And BackTracker failed.

-

The Power of A Product Strategy

But why can product strategy be so powerful when we get it right?

When teaching aspiring product leaders about product strategy, I refer to product strategy as the following:

"The one decision which solves a thousand decisions"

Why?

Whether you are a Product Manager, or working in a more senior product role, ultimately your purpose is to mitigate risk.

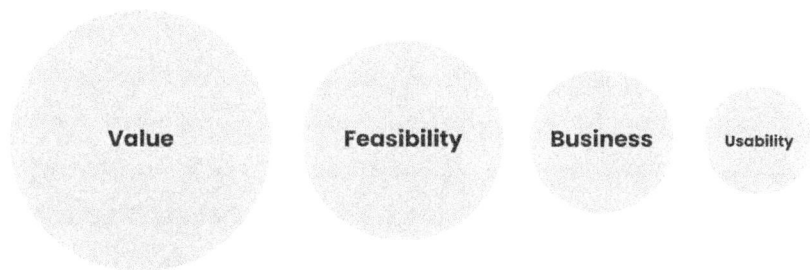

Specifically, 4 types of risk:

1. **Value risk**: Does our market actually want this?
2. **Feasibility risk**: Can we actually build this?
3. **Usability risk**: Can they actually use it?

4. **Business risk**: Is this thing relevant to our business to work on?

In most companies, product teams usually focus most of their attention on Feasibility risk i.e. working out *how* to build something.

Here's the thing:

That's not your priority[1].

Your priority is value risk.

Why?

You could have the best user experience, the most scalable code & the greatest functionality.

But if you are working on something that your target market doesn't care about, it's all a waste of time.

It simply doesn't matter.

As a product leader, you must therefore obsess over answering that one essential question before worrying about *what* specific solution to build & *how* to build it:

---

[1] It **might** be in a few specific situations. Example: You work with a world-class product discovery team and/or have strongly validated a solution through testing & iterating different prototypes.

Does our market actually want this?

Furthermore, answering this question becomes even more important every single year.

Why? There are more than 10x the number of websites online than their were just 10 years ago. That means 10x the number of products available, which in turn means 10x the competition.

Unlike 2008, when the Lean Startup was published & the emphasis was on simply to "build something, launch it & see what happens", you need to be far more strategic about what you can offer your market that will be genuinely *unique* & genuinely *valuable*.

As Marty Cagan states,

> "First, you need to discover whether there are real users out there that want this product… Second, you need to discover a product solution to this problem that is usable, useful, and feasible."

That doesn't mean we need to build a full solution & show it to our target customer straight away in order to mitigate value risk.

Not at all.

Instead, we can answer that question by making a simple promise - outlining our value proposition (which in turn reflects the core of our product strategy) - and seeing how our target market reacts.

But more on that in the following chapters.

Let us, for now, come back to why product strategy is so important:

Why, then, do we at Prod MBA refer to product strategy as "the one decision to solve a thousand decisions"?

Two key reasons:

1. To validate what we should focus on

If you are able to present your product strategy to your target market & see that they value what you are offering, then it shows you that you are focusing on the right thing/s.

This means, when you come to working out what to build, you can be confident that anything that will help you deliver on your unique value proposition has as good a chance of success as possible.

Coming back to our Prod MBA example, if we know that our target market values "hands-on" and "actionable" learning, then we can be confident focusing on any ideas & solutions that will help us deliver more "hands-on" and "actionable" learning - & ignore everything else.

2. To convince stakeholders of what we should focus on

Understanding & validating product strategy is a powerful first step. But it is not enough within the context of a company.

Instead, you also need to get stakeholders on board to *agree* with what you should - and should not - focus on.

Aligning around a shared product strategy statement is a powerful way of getting stakeholders to be part of decision-making process & buy into that product strategy.

And that's why we call a great product strategy "the one decision to resolve a thousand decisions":

It validates what you should focus on, & aligns stakeholders around what you should focus on, thus nullifying the principle villains of any product team:

Endless meetings, back-and-forth discussions, irrelevant product ideas popping up, misalignment, inability to prioritise, lack of focus, internal conflict, etc.

But enough of the theory.

Shall we get started learning how to actually *craft* a great product strategy?

It all starts with finding a real problem to solve.

Starting With The Right Foundations: Problems

It's a cliché in product to say, "Start with the problem."

And, in most cases, it's bad & very dangerous advice.

Because in many cases, product teams don't actually know what "the problem" really is, nor how to think about problems!

I've observed this myself hundreds of times.

At the beginning of our Prod MBA bootcamp, for example, students are tasked with building a real product from scratch.

This process starts with them identifying a problem to solve.

Yet 90% make the same mistake.

Take Joe, as just one example.

In our first coaching session, Joe was excited.

"*I've discovered this huge problem & I've got the **PERFECT** solution to solve it as well. It's going to be big.*"

So I asked him, "*Well, what's the problem then?*"

"*That current calendar apps are just confusing & not interactive enough.*"

"*Ok...*", I said. "*So **why** is that a problem?*"

A blank stare came back at me.

With hesitation in his voice, Joe replied, "Well... Calendar apps should be easy to use..."

Joe wasn't wrong. I'm sure his research was more or less correct! I'm sure there are many people who find current calendar apps confusing!

The problem?

He had identified a **symptom**, *not* the **root cause** of the problem.

I.E. WHY is it important that these people use a calendar in the first place?!

The root of the problem?

People struggle to manage their time effectively.

Surface-Level Problem

"Calendar apps are confusing"

Root Problem

"People struggle to manage their time effectively"

A calendar app is just *one* way of attempting to solve that problem (managing their time effectively).

Yet there are many *other ways* people do - or could - manage their time effectively.

They could focus on how they plan their day, or writing a morning journal, or meditating, or changing to a less busy job, as just a few examples.

Now Joe could get lucky.

He could zoom in on that symptom of the root problem (how to build a less confusing calendar). He could build something people love. Something he and his team could even make money from!

However, what happens if his hypothesis is wrong?

What happens if building "a better calendar" just isn't something people want? Or Joe doesn't really know what kind of "better" he should deliver? Or it's unfeasible for his team to build?

What then?

If we aren't clear what the root problem is that we are solving, we will never know what to pivot to when our hypotheses are (inevitably) proven wrong.

We will simply flail around, trying different solutions to non-problems.

And - trust me from experience plus studies conducted on product success - that is a certain path to failure.

How to Find The Right Problem to Solve?

Selecting the right problem to solve in product is half of the battle.

If we start with the right problem, it is far easier to attract our target market, to convert them to users, and to get them to pay for our product.

There are 4 specific questions we want to ask ourselves when assessing whether we should explore solving a specific problem:

1. Is the problem acute?
2. Is the market addressable?
3. Are we intrinsically motivated to solve this problem?

4. What is the market potential?

Is The Problem Acute?

Firstly, you want to assess whether the problem is acute for your target customer.

An easy question to ask yourself is:

Would a solution here be a **vitamin** (i.e. helps a little bit) or a **pain-killer** (i.e. something that would bring a lot of relief & solves an urgent problem)?

If the problem isn't something your target market thinks about daily - something that keeps them up at night, even - then it will be a lot harder to attract them, to convert them to users, and to charge them for your product.

Why?

Because the problem just isn't a priority for them!

They won't bother putting the time & effort into trying your new product - even if it's a free product.

One of our students, Nitin, for example, could tell very quickly that he had discovered an acute problem:

When speaking to his target customers to understand the problem more, he had people visibly angry on the phone to him! They were so frustrated with the process of selecting the right healthcare option that his calls - calls with complete strangers - were lasting over an hour each time!

(Not all products need to solve acute problems, by the way. However, a solution to a non-acute problem must be unbelievably simple & effortless.

I don't have an urgent need to use Google Search when I want to look up who played in the 2002 World Cup Final, for example, but the solution is so simple & so effective that the lower motivation I may have to use the product - based on having a less acute problem - is counteracted by how simple the product is to use.)

Is the market addressable?

Secondly, you need to be able to actually find & access those who have the problem.

You could have the best product in the world, but if it's not getting in front of the right target market, then nobody will use it, and your product will fail.

It's therefore essential to prove that you can find your market.

That could be by discovering where they hang out (e.g. physical locations like a bar, or online spaces like forums) or creating a proven way to attract that group to you (e.g. a blog or LinkedIn posts).

Are we intrinsically motivated to solve this problem?

Thirdly, you need to actually be interested in the problem & motivated to try to solve it!

Product is a game of persistence &, using the words of Winston Churchill, success stems from *"the ability to go from one failure to another with no loss of enthusiasm"*.

The endless hours of speaking to customers, the disappointment of a failed experiment, the countless hours thinking about the problem, the difficult conversations with stakeholders...

All of these things are made infinitely harder when you are not deeply motivated to solve the problem.

What is the market potential?

Finally, although you don't want to make the classic mistake of many MBA students & universities of over-analysing a market, you do want to have a rough idea of the long-term potential.

To do so, you can look at:

a) **The ability to branch out** into other customer segments and/or opportunity spaces. For example, you might start by helping *busy CEOs* "manage their time more effectively", but later help *other* professionals, or even try to solve *another* problem for our busy CEOs

b) **Spend per customer:** It's worth looking at what this target customer tends to spend to solve this problem already. Although you should eventually present a very different solution to what already exists (more on this in following chapters), this will give you an idea of spending power, thus potentially making it easier for you to achieve profitability

c) **Heuristics:** You can look at the kind of behaviours & beliefs of this target customer to either leverage or counter. For example, it is a "heuristic" (norm) that tech companies use some sort of channel-based communications platform (e.g. Slack, Microsoft Teams). If you are thinking of launching a competitor in this space, you might integrate the heuristic of "channels" to your proposed solution so that you reduce friction for those teams & are more easily able to help them switch to your new product

d) **Persistent Trends:** You should also consider what trends you think will be short-term v. Long-term. During Covid lockdowns, for example, there were many changes in behaviour, such as people not spending a penny in pubs & bars. Was that something that would likely persist? No. Was working from home likely to persist? Yes, to a large extent. Therefore, you would want to plan around a long-term trend, such as "work from home", to ensure your product strategy *remains* relevant.

Finally, when selecting the right problem, perhaps the most important point is this:

You can NEVER know that we have selected the *perfect* problem.

You can do some analysis. You can ask the right questions. But you can never predict the market.

My advice?

Just pick one.

Then go & actually *speak* to your target market to answer the following:

Is this a *real, acute* problem?

How to answer that question? That will be the subject of the next chapter.

Bonus: How To Generate Ideas for Problems

The focus of *this* book is on how to define a product strategy, *not* how to come up with a great business idea.

However, it's worth mentioning the 4 specific tactics we suggest students use to generate ideas for problems (problems being the core around which we build a product to solve):

1. **You & your friends:** Simply list down any problems you have encountered in the last month. Alternatively, outsource it by speaking to friends & colleagues about problems they've faced, or simply post on any communities you are a part of
2. **Forums:** Browse existing communities you are a part of, or browse Facebook, Reddit, etc., for suggested communities. If they are being suggested, it's likely they are active and/or growing communities
3. **Google Trends:** Enter keywords into trends.google.com to discover whether there has been an increase in search terms over the last few months or years. A simple example: Imagine you searched "how to improve my immune system" in March 2020 & saw a huge increase in searches for this term. It may have triggered you to build a product in this space
4. **Keyword analysis (advanced):** You can use tools like www.ahrefs.com to enter a specific search term (such as "content marketing") & it will show you how competitive those terms are, as well as, more importantly for this exercise, related searches & keywords. These can be a great source of ideas for problems to solve

Putting This Into Practice

The foundation of any good product strategy is a clear definition of the problem.

Therefore, in one sentence, what is the problem you are solving?

Example: *"It's hard to manage your time properly at work."*

DEFINE PROBLEM

"It's hard to manage your time properly at work."

Starting With The Right Foundations: Niches

The traditional approach to building a successful business is outdated.

Particularly with regard to how you should think about selecting your target market.

Traditional business theory teaches that we should go for the broadest market possible. To try to capture as many potential customers as possible. Because a broader market = more potential users. More users = more potential revenue.

Yet **this approach can undermine success right from the start**.

Furthermore, many product teams simply come up with a solution & don't even *think* about the target audience.

They may be working on some new, exciting technology. Or they fall into the trap of trying to target as broad a group as possible. Or they simply don't speak to enough potential customers to understand what their true needs are.

Whatever the reason, as Seth Godin states,

> "You can't come up with a product or service and THEN decide to market it."

This is a guaranteed path to building a product nobody wants.

In fact, almost all successful products started with a very small, very specific audience.

They succeeded by focusing on what we call a niche: A specific, distinct group of people to serve. When Facebook started, it was exclusively for Harvard students. When Stripe started, it was only for backend developers. When Miro started, it was only for Product Managers looking to improve online collaboration.

Facebook Early Niche

Total Harvard Students

A small, specific audience means we are more likely to succeed.

Why?

Because a small, specific audience means we can focus *just* on that group & the unique problem that *they* need solved.

Furthermore, the more specific our audience, the better.

Because the more specific we are, the more likely we are to build something truly valuable for the specific, unique needs of that audience. Let me illustrate the point:

Imagine you are a first-time startup founder walking down a busy street. One company shouts across the crowd,

"Hey, startup founders! We built this new thing for you!"

You might pay attention. You might not. But there are a lot of startup founders in the world, so is it likely something specifically for you? Probably not.

Imagine another company now shouts across the crowd,

"Hey, **first-time** startup founder! We know how **uncertain** & **intimidating** those first few months can be. We know it can be **overwhelming**. We built this new thing for you!"

Who would you pay more attention to?

That second company, of course. Why? Because they are demonstrating that they understand that you have *unique* problems to solve that are very *specific* to *your* unique situation (i.e. as an overwhelmed, first-time founder, rather than just any startup founder).

Therefore, the more specific you can be in who we target, the better. Because you are more likely to attract them & more likely to build the right, unique product to solve their problems.

There are countless examples of successful businesses that focus on a very specific target audience.

The [Handcrafted Soap & Cosmetic Guild](), for example, organises a conference for 450 people annually - enough to sustain itself as a successful business.

There's [another company]() which makes millions selling raised dog beds to keep your dog cool.

Another company, [Nomadlist](), run by one person, makes $1m+ in revenue from helping digital nomads find their next place to live.

Success for all these companies stems from being very specific in who their product is for - & executing to deliver for that specific audience.

That's not to say that we should never broaden our target audience. Most companies will - & should - scale to other audiences.

Facebook, for example, eventually targeted any & *everyone*. Stripe is now used by *anyone* wanting to handle digital payments. Miro is used by *anyone* looking to create & collaborate online.

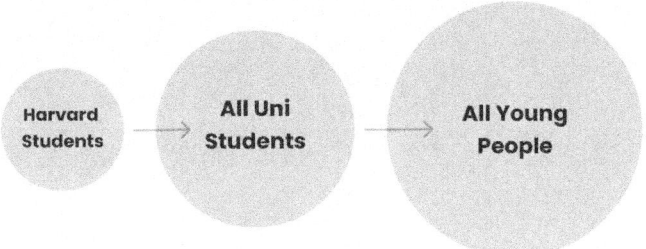

However, we must be disciplined in finding a specific audience to serve. Disciplined in working out what to deliver to that audience. And disciplined in executing to actually deliver a lot of value to that audience. Only once we have some level of Product-Market Fit[2] (lots

---

[2] "Product-market fit describes a scenario in which a company's target customers are buying, using, and telling others about the company's product in numbers large enough to sustain that product's growth and profitability. According to entrepreneur and investor Marc Andreesen, who is often credited with developing the concept, product-market fit means finding a good market with a product capable of satisfying that market." - Product-Market Fit, ProductPlan

of users, users sticking around, revenue coming in, etc.), should we think about broadening to other markets.

Because we do want to deliver value for as big an audience as possible. Eventually. However, to get there, we need to be very focused to start.

How to Define Your Target Market

Step 1: Define The Problem

In order to define *who* we should build our product for, we must start with the problem.

As outlined in the previous chapter, that means coming up with a hypothesis about what the specific problem is that you want to solve - & determining what the true problem really is.

Continuing with our example from the last chapter, let's say the problem statement we are exploring is this:

"People struggle with managing their time."

In fact, in reality, we are likely to start a bit more specific, outlining a broad market we think the problem applies to:

"**People working in startups** struggle to manage their time."

Step 2: Be More Specific

Now that we have a problem to focus on, we need to focus on a specific target audience who we believe suffers from this problem.

"People working in startups" is not specific. It is too broad.

What do we mean by *"people working in startups"*? Does that include *everyone* working in *every* startup? Every *role*? Every *stage* of startup? Every *type of need* related to time management?

Instead, we need to ask ourselves:

For whom is this problem of "managing one's time" **most** *acute for?*

To start, we could think of demographic characteristics to be more specific.

For example, does the specific role matter? In this case, yes. That would be a fair hypothesis. For a busy CEO of an early-stage startup, time management is likely a very acute issue. For a Junior Sales Rep, time management probably isn't that big a priority (making sales by changing their sales tactics, for example, would be more important).

In this case, we could look at the type of role, gender, age, company stage, etc., to try to define a more specific group.

Even better though, would be to focus on psychographic characteristics to be both more specific & to find the most acute niche to focus on.

To do so, we want to look at the psychology of the person we are looking to help. Are they stressed? Under pressure? Struggling with some particularly difficult challenge?

We want to really get in their head & *empathise* with what they are going through emotionally.

Looking through a psychographic lens, for example, we might hypothesis that time management is more acute for startup teams *when they are trying to raise investment* (as they need to demonstrate strong results, therefore needing to be more productive). It also might be more acute for those working in an *early-stage* startup v. A *mature* startup, where there is massive uncertainty & a need to find Product-Market Fit to trigger sustained growth.

Having thought through demographic & psychographic factors that might be relevant, we might, in this case settle on a more specific niche in the belief that time management is a very acute problem for them:

Startup *founders* (rather than just *anyone* working in a startup).

Step 3: Be As Specific As Possible!

Once you have been more specific in who you want to build your product for, you need to push yourself to be even more specific!

To do so, simply ask yourself:

If I could pick a group of maximum 100 people, how would I define them?

There are likely tens of thousands of startup founders in the world, for example. It's therefore too broad still.

Instead, you might define your initial market very specifically, like so:

Founders of **early-stage** startups **in London** raising their **first round of investment**.

Why? Because your hypothesis is that:

- Early-stage startups are very chaotic & require a huge amount of work
- You might start in London because you have a network there, or you know where to find London startup founders
- You may specifically target those raising their first round of investment because you know that doing so will put extra pressure on their time, as well as pressure on their team to deliver results

All of these factors contribute to the problem of "time management" seeming *extremely* acute for this specific niche.

3 Niche Levels

INITIAL NICHE

People working in a startup

↓

2ND LEVEL NICHE

Startup founders

↓

3RD LEVEL NICHE

Founders of early-stage startups in London raising their first round of investment

Finally, by being very specific to start, it does not mean we are closing the door to other niches.

It simply means we are focusing on that specific niche to start, before broadening out as our product gets traction.

Furthermore, in many cases, there may be many, seemingly equally acute niches to try to serve (for example, you might see a problem as very acute for both startup founders & startup Product Managers). Just pick *one* to start & pivot if needed as you start validating the problem.

Putting This Into Practice

You can use the following, simple table to define different possible niches to build your product for:

1. Define the problem
2. Define who, broadly, you think the problem is relevant for (Level 1 Niche)
3. Define a more specific niche, who you think the problem is more acute for (Level 2 Niche)
4. Define as specific a niche as possible, who you think the problem is most acute for (Level 3 Niche)
5. Justify your decision by adding an "Acuteness" score. 1 = not very acute, 5 = is so acute it keeps them up at night

DEFINE PROBLEM

INITIAL NICHE

ACUTENESS

/5

↓

2ND LEVEL NICHE

ACUTENESS

/5

↓

3RD LEVEL NICHE

ACUTENESS

/5

We suggest to students defining 10-20 different, unrelated problem statements & niches before committing to product discovery work.

In the context of a company, you should do the same, with the ideas you generate related to your business goals.

Conclusion

A specific problem & niche are the foundations for the success of our product. And the foundations for our product strategy.

In the long-term, the goal of our product strategy is to build something specific for our niche. By doing so, we want to convert that niche target customer into a "High Experience Customer":

Those from within our niche who demonstrably derive clear value from our product I.E. they are signing up for our product, sticking with our product, paying for our product, & referring others from the niche to our product.

But we can only achieve that by building the right foundations. By building the right product strategy.

And doing so starts with selecting the right problem, selecting the specific niche we think the problem is most acute for, then doing the product discovery work to see whether the problem is in fact *real* & what specific *value* we should provide for our niche.

(Note: Before you move onto the next chapter, it's worth re-visiting your problem statement & the specific niche you believe the problem is most relevant for. You could also run a workshop with your team to define different possible problem statements, before agreeing upon a final statement.)

How to Discover Your Product Strategy: The 4 Stages

There is a very dangerous myth in the world of product strategy.

One that is pushed by traditional MBA programmes, consultancy firms & many investors.

It constitutes THE biggest mistake product teams make when trying to come up with a great product strategy:

Thinking that doing competitor analysis will magically help you discover a great product strategy.

Here's the reality:

Having a brainstorming session & writing out all the pros & cons of your potential competitors rarely works.

Why?

Because we need *unique insights* to drive a product strategy:

Maybe an original approach to the problem that questions convention. Maybe some new technology that means we can solve a problem better and/or faster. Maybe just focusing on doing one thing 10x better than anyone else.

Unique insights rarely come from discussing the problem as a group. Instead, unique insights come from actually getting out the building & speaking to your niche!

Take the example of Superhuman again:

Their obsessive focus on speed - being the "fastest ever email experience" - didn't come from sitting in a conference room analysing all the pros & cons of Gmail. It came from a *sense* that email was problematic for their niche (busy startup leaders).

That *sense* was then confirmed by product discovery: Actually speaking to busy startup leaders to understand what the problems were related to using email. By doing so, they discovered that unique insight that now drives everything they do:

That email was taking up too much time each day for their niche.

Or take our example at Prod MBA:

We didn't start out by analysing all the product books, courses & consultants out there to magically come up with the idea for our product.

Instead, we started with a *sense* that existing solutions didn't seem to be helping product people skill-up effectively. We therefore immediately started speaking to Product Managers with 0-2 years experience (the group we felt suffered most acutely & who were most addressable). From speaking to those Product Managers, it became clear that books, YouTube videos & online courses were "too theoretical" and they lacked "effective support & mentorship."

That *sense*, once validated with real target customers, became *insight* backed up by qualitative data.

Of those insights, we focused on the *unique* insight that now drive everything we do: providing the most "hands-on" & "actionable" product career training in the market by getting students to build a real product from zero to revenue.

This is not to say that analysing the competition is not important.

It is.

However, it is simply a step that must come *later* in the process of discovering a great product strategy.

(Discovery being the key word here, as a great product strategy is something that takes time - and numerous interactions with our niche - to develop.)

To discover a great product strategy, we must go through each stage of the following process, in the correct order:

1. **Stage 1:** Speak to our target customer to understand the problem better

2. **Stage 2:** Assess whether the problem is real and/or acute, as well as identify specific opportunities related to the problem. This will drive our product vision & strategy
3. **Stage 3:** Analyse competitors & existing alternatives to see whether we do, in fact, have something unique to offer
4. **Stage 4:** Craft a great product strategy statement to pitch to our niche, as well as to align our team internally

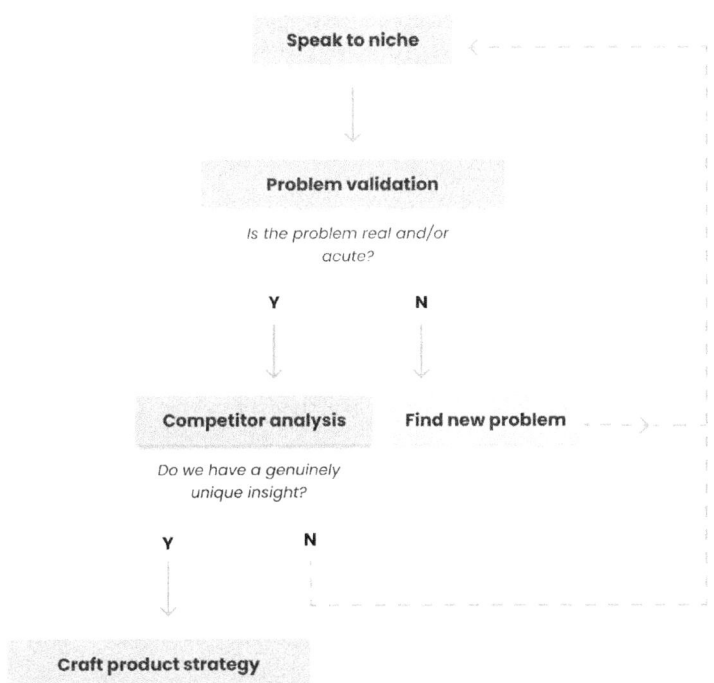

How to Discover Your Product Strategy: Discovery Calls

During our Prod MBA bootcamp, once students have defined the problem they want to solve, & the niche they want to solve it for, they fall into the following trap:

They get over-excited.

They think it's the biggest problem in the world.

They are convinced it's going to be the next big thing.

And they start to visualise what the solution will be, down to the very features & individual screens that will make up that solution.

This is where we as mentors step in - & tell them to stop!

Why?

Everything is still an *assumption* at this stage. We don't know:

- **Is the problem a *real* problem?**
- **Is it relevant and/or acute for *this niche*?**
- **Is it an *acute enough* problem to be worth solving?**

Rather than sitting & staring at those questions, or sitting around a conference room to magically come up with the answers, instead, you need to speak to your niche to discover answers to these key questions.

And even when you do speak to our niche, you may discover that the problem is not in fact that acute (meaning you might want to pivot to another problem), or you may not have any idea about how you we might solve the problem - or you may realise that there's another problem more acute for you to solve!

My point?

Product discovery is hard. There's a 50+% chance our hypotheses are wrong & it rarely gives us a clear answer/s to our key hypotheses[3].

But it must be done. Because without speaking to our target customer early on, we set ourselves up for failure:

Committing time, money & resources to a problem that doesn't need solving.

---

[3] Based on my anecdotal experience training nearly 300 Product Managers in product discovery.

How to Conduct an Effective Discovery Call

A discovery call is a conversation with an existing user, or a target user, with the objective of trying to elicit a deeper understanding of the problem space we are exploring.

We call them "discovery calls" and not "user interviews" because the emphasis should be on *discovery* i.e. we should go into each call open-minded, curious & without any fixed assumptions about the problem space, with the goal of uncovering - discovering - something we did know before.

In this section, I will explain how you run an effective discovery call in order to uncover the kind of unique insights needed to drive a winning product strategy.

There are 4 steps we will cover:

1. How to find candidates for a discovery call
2. The Discovery Call Script
3. Tips & tactics for conducting an effective discovery call
4. Preparing for your discovery calls

(Note: I won't go into a lot of depth around how to conduct discovery calls effectively, as this is a book on product strategy, not product discovery. For further reading, *The Mom Test* does an excellent job of covering the do's & don'ts of speaking to your target users & will only take you 3-4hrs to read the entire book. Teresa Torres' *Continuous Discovery* is also a great book on product discovery.)

Step 1: Finding candidates

For Existing Products

If you have an existing user base, finding candidates is usually very easy.

Reach out directly to users in your database who you feel fit your target audience. You may, for example, want to target regular users of your product, or those who you know fit a certain psychographic (e.g. "overwhelmed" founders) or demographic (e.g. "Product Manager with 2 years experience").

Once you've identified your targets, reach out to them with a simple, clear message. You can support this with some sort of incentive to join a call, such a free Amazon voucher.

Here's a template you can customise to your context:

"Hi John, I'm reaching out to you as we are looking for feedback in order to improve [insert product's name].

All I need is 15-20 mins of your time to ask you some questions about [insert the problem you are solving]. We'll give you a $20 Amazon voucher as a thank you straight after the call!

Would you be interested in having a quick call this week?"

If you get a positive response, simply send them a link to book a call with you (we use Calendly to do so, which also automatically creates a Zoom link for them to use for the call).

For existing products, you can generally be more direct, as the user recognises (& hopefully trusts) your brand, so, in most cases, will be more willing to help.

New Products

If you are developing a new product & have no existing users, finding the right candidates requires a little more work.

Your starting point should be to ask yourself:

Where does my niche hang out?

Think back to the chapter on finding the right problem. You will remember that one of the key factors in choosing the right problem was "addressability" i.e. can we actually *find* our target niche?

It might be in specific online forums, such as Facebook or Reddit, or you may find your niche hangs out more in-person, such as at a "Product Manager's Meetup" in Central London.

Once you discover where they hang out, it's time to reach out to them.

Whether you need to reach out to your niche on LinkedIn, Reddit, Instagram or whatever online platform, the same principles apply when reaching out:

1. **Create trust with the community**, through posting new questions, answers to community questions, interesting articles, etc. Write 2-3 posts per week for at least 2 weeks to truly build trust & visibility
2. Once your name is recognised & trusted, you can **reach out directly** to those in your target group. We suggest reaching out to 40-50 people at least, as many simply are not active on the platform, are busy, or think you are a spammer.
3. **If a connection is required**, such as on LinkedIn, to reach out, **use a "soft connect" message**: Simply add them with no direct request in order to not coming across immediately like you are selling them something e.g.

   "Hi John, I noticed you're also active in [community name]. Thought it would be nice to connect, Henry"

4. Once a connection has been requested, **follow up with a direct request** to book a call with you:

   "Hi John, I'm reaching out to you as we're building a product to solve [insert problem you are solving].

   I'd really appreciate 15-20 mins of your time to ask you some questions about [the problem] to understand it better.

   Would you be interested in having a quick call this week?"

The specific message, sequence of messages, etc., will depend on the platform. However, try to stick to these principles.

If, on the other hand, you are dealing with a physical community, such as at an in-person Meetup, you can simply conduct the discovery calls informally, as a conversation!

When I worked in travel, I would walk every single week to a hostel nearby in order to speak to potential users, as well as test out new prototype iterations. The feedback was absolutely invaluable - and fun!

Step 2: Using The Right Script**

For each discovery call, you want to follow the right script. A script designed to help you dig under the surface to uncover truly unique insights about your niche & the problem space.

To start the call, you should use a scripted introduction in order to move from general chit-chat to the substance - the questions - in the script.

Remember, you aren't here to chat about the weather, or hear about how their cat needs to go to the vet later. You are here to uncover unique insights.

We therefore suggest using the following introduction when they join the call:

You: "Hi John, how's it going?"

John: "Good thanks. You?"

You: "Good good, thanks! Well... Shall I start by giving you a bit of info on why I wanted to speak to you today?"

John: "Sure..."

You: "Great. I wanted to meet just to ask you a few questions about [insert problem they face]. We're developing a product to solve this, but want to better understand some of the challenges you face related to [the problem], how you've tried to solve it before, etc. It should only take 20 minutes or so. Are you happy to get started?"

John: "Ok. Sure."

You: "Great. So..."

Clearly not every conversation will follow this *exact* format, but, however the conversation starts. Adapt based on what is in front of you on the call.

The core principle behind the script, however, should be followed; that means you want to *quickly* move from a greeting to an overview of what you will cover, then to get permission to start before you jump into your questions.

Once you have completed your scripted introduction, you can then ask the key questions from our script:

1. **Could you tell me a little bit about [the problem]?** Here we are trying to understand whether this problem is in fact something they face

2. **What is the main challenge you are facing at the moment in relation to [the problem]?** Here we are trying to sense whether the problem is real & acute, as well as to uncover some of the nuances of the problem space
3. **How have you tried to solve this before?** Here we are trying to get a concrete answer to whether the problem is acute. If they have committed time, money and/or energy to trying to solve it, then it's a good sign this is an acute problem
4. **What has prevented you solving [the problem] in the past?** Here we are trying to uncover potential beliefs & habits related to the problem. By understanding these, we may get ideas about how we could eventually solve the problem
5. **If you had a magic wand, how would you ideal solve this?** Here we are simply generating ideas of how we might solve the problem (or generating insights by trying to understand why they might have suggested a certain idea)

Once you've asked all of your key questions - as well as any follow-up questions you might think of - you want to move to a clear next step with the interviewee.

To do so, you can finish the call with the following:

You: *"That was super helpful, John. I've got some great ideas from our conversation to go & work on with the team. Just a final question: Would you be willing to have another call in a few weeks to test our solution?"*

If they agree, you want to book a time with them on the call, so there is some commitment. Each interviewee is a potential early user, so this is a great way to save time finding new leads. It's also a good indication that the problem is acute if they are willing to commit more time to help you!

Step 3: Tips & Tactics

When you conduct a discovery call, it is essential that you bear in mind the following tips & tactics:

1. **Keep the conversation open:** Despite having a script, you want to see where the interviewee might lead the conversation. Maybe there is a specific challenge they face that you want to dig into more & ask follow-up questions. Or maybe they have a completely unrelated problem you weren't aware of that is more acute to solve. Deep insights come from going *deep* on a conversation & *digging in with follow-up questions*. That's usually where the non-obvious, unique insights lie, so you want to stay open to where the conversation may go
2. **Ask all your key questions:** On the other hand, you *do* want to ask all of the questions from your script. Why? It's easier to quantify your results at the end of a batch of interviews if all interviewees responded to the same questions, making our learnings more actionable (e.g. "80% of interviewees mentioned they struggled with X..."). It also means you can come out of a batch of interviews able to answer your key hypotheses around whether the problem is real and/or whether it is acute in a methodical way. The key is to thread the scripted questions naturally into the conversation (something that comes with practice!)
3. **Ask past-based questions:** Avoid any hypothetical questions (e.g. "*Would* you pay for this product?") because interviewees will not give you an accurate answer. Either they will deliberately lie to be polite to you, or they simply don't know what they *would* do in a hypothetical situation. Regardless, you want to base answers on facts. The best way to get facts is to ask questions based on past behaviour (e.g. "*Have* you spent any money *in the last 6 months* to try to solve this problem?")
4. **Have a call-to-action:** Always finish with a clear next step! That could be asking them to book another call in with you, or asking for an introduction from someone else they might

know in your niche. Don't waste these rare opportunities to access your niche!

Step 4: Preparing For a Discovery Call

The goal is to repeat reaching out to your target user until you have 12-13 discovery calls booked in.

Ideally you want to conduct at least 10 calls in order to start recognising trends & patterns in those calls. However, expect 10-20% to not turn up to the call or to cancel, due to busyness or forgetfulness. Therefore best to book in a few extra calls.

In terms of preparation, we suggest using the following [Miro template](#) for your batch of discovery calls:

Interview Notes	Interviewee Name	Interviewee Name	Interviewee Name	Interviewee Name
Tell me a little bit about yourself/the problem				
What is the main challenge you are facing at the moment in relation to [problem]?				
How have you tried to solve this before?				
What has prevented you solving [problem] in the past?				

Why is this template so important?

A few reasons:

1. **Lean Note-Taking:** Teams that take copious notes, or record a discovery call, rarely actually come back to review the notes or recording afterwards. It just takes up too much time. Therefore, it is far more realistic to note down just the key points from the conversation
2. **Remove Friction:** *Ideally* you conduct each discovery call with one person conducting the interview & the other taking notes. However, this isn't always possible. Considering you should be speaking to at least 5 people from our niche every single week, you need to remove any excuses & any friction. You must be prepared to conduct discovery calls by yourself if necessary. The structure of the script & simplicity of this note-taking format empower you to conduct a call alone when needed
3. **Visibility:** Most companies do not understand the value of product discovery. You therefore need to make sure it is easy for stakeholders to quickly scan notes & take away the key learnings (thus helping them see the value in product discovery). Following a uniform approach to note-taking, noting down just the highlights & having these on a shared Miro is the best way to achieve this
4. **Quantifying Qualitative Data:** Perhaps the most important reason to use this template is that, by noting down key highlights from our 10+ discovery calls, we are able to draw connections between key themes that emerge. This in turn helps us to quantify the data, demonstrating to stakeholders which themes & frustrations are most acute & for what percentage of our target users they are relevant for. Rather than trying to present just a mass of notes, instead, we have clear, quantified themes to present to stakeholders - far more effective at influencing their decision-making than a mass of qualitative data

How To Use The Template

This template is designed for you to add notes from your discovery call all in one place.

The template itself should be prepared before your first discovery call. To do so, simply download the Miro board (you can do so here) & copy it to your own Miro account.

Using the template is simple. Before the call, add some details of the person you are interviewing at the top so you can identify later who it was:

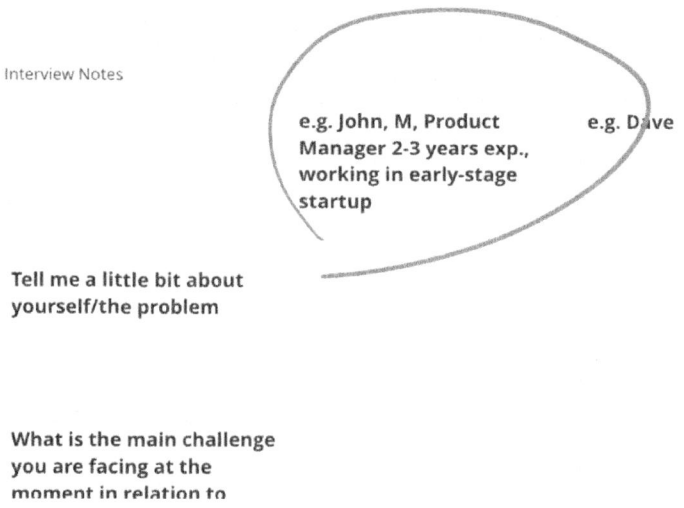

When you then start, as you go through each question in your discovery call script, add 2-3 key highlights from that question in the box provided. These could be exact quotes from the interviewee, your own observations, or key points they made. An example:

Interview Notes

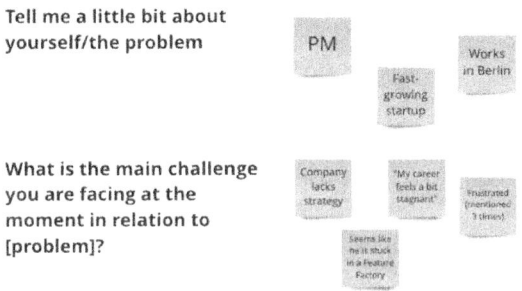

After the call, you should end up with a column full of key highlights, like the one below. To wrap up, you can add any final notes or comments at the bottom, like so:

But what do we actually do with all these notes?! And how in any way are they related to product strategy?

Let's jump into that now, in the next chapter.

How to Craft Your Product Strategy: Identifying Opportunities

Once we have conducted our discovery calls, we should have a much deeper understanding of the problem space.

With that deeper understanding, we are now able to answer the following key hypotheses:

1. Is the problem real?
2. Is the problem acute?
3. Is it acute enough to be worth solving?
4. What specific opportunities can we identify related to the problem?

Is the problem real?

As I mentioned in the chapter on "The Problem", in most cases we usually have a good sense of whether the problem is, in fact, a real problem.

However, we likely lack depth to that understanding.

For example, from the discovery calls we may realise that we weren't exploring the true problem. We might, for example, have started asking our niche about their struggles "finding the right diet", when the real problem is in fact "helping them achieve their dream body".

Or we may in fact realise that this simply isn't a real problem. That our initial hunch was wrong.

Unfortunately there is no definitive way to say, "Yes, this is a real problem". The key indicator is whether they have committed at least *some* time, effort and/or money to trying to solve the problem before.

If yes, it shows this is something they consider a problem & have attempted to solve. If not, you may want to find another problem to solve.

Is the problem acute?

From your discovery calls, you should now have a clear sense of whether the problem is in fact acute or not.

If there's evidence that the niche has committed **significant** money, time and/or effort to solving the problem, then we can be confident that the problem is acute.

Or we may uncover some deep negative beliefs & habits that have made them simply give up on solving it; think of our dieting example above, where people who struggle with weight loss have all sorts of negative beliefs, conflicting data & bad experiences around dieting.

The hard part?

We can't really *quantify* acuteness! We can't say, "well, our niche spent $100 on average this month trying to solve it, so it's definitely acute." It really just depends on each unique problem & a *sense* we get from speaking to so many people from our niche, from their past behaviour & from the emotions we pick up from them on the call.

Is it acute enough to be worth solving?

Once we get a sense for how acute the problem is, we are faced with the following question:

Do we pivot to another problem, or persist & try to solve it?

There's no easy answer to this question. It depends on the specific problem space you are exploring. In some cases, we can build a hugely successful product for a non-acute problem (remember my Google Search example). I suggest only pursuing a non-acute problem if you have a clear idea of a very simple, very effective & unique way of solving the problem that nobody else has built before. This is usually 1) hard to come up with, or others would have done it and 2) risky, as it's much harder to pivot on the problem once you've committed to a solution.

If you **do** think you've discovered an acute problem to solve, the next step is to think about how you might approach solving it.

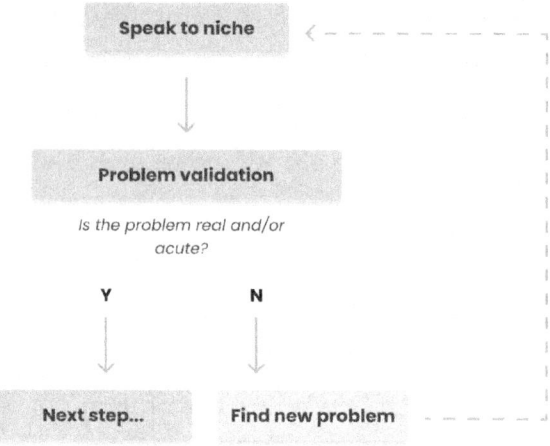

What specific opportunities can we identify related to the problem?

Once we decide that yes, this is the right problem for us to solve, we need to identify specific opportunities we see in the market to help build a great product strategy.

But what do I mean by "opportunities"?

Opportunities, in the context of product discovery, are specific areas of value that we could focus on.

This might be a *single* opportunity.

For example, for Superhuman, it was a realisation that the key insight from people they interviewed for their discovery calls was that email took up "too much time". 2-3 hours per day to be specific. Superhuman's decision to focus on "speed" was an opportunity that they wanted to take advantage of, with the hope that focusing on this opportunity (more speed) would deliver lots of value to their users. By delivering lots of value to their users, they hoped to then capture some of that value for the business in the form of revenue (and, ideally, profit).

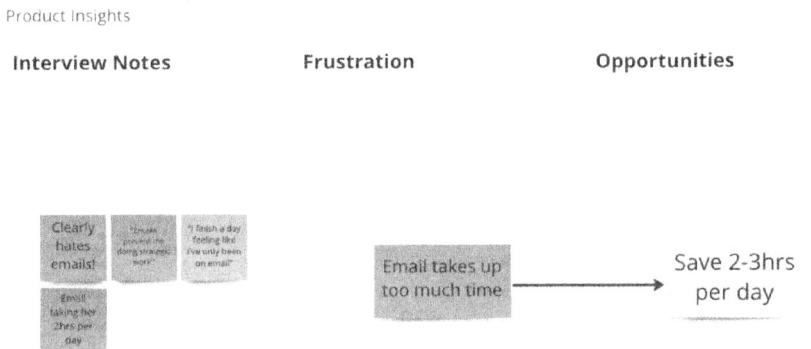

In contrast, you can focus on *multiple* opportunities. Take Prod MBA:

We identified that "courses & books were *too theoretical*" and that there was a "lack of *mentorship*" for Product Managers trying to accelerate their career growth.

We therefore tried to address both opportunities in our initial solution, focusing on flipping these problems:

The problem of resources being "too theoretical" meant we promised to be "extremely hands-on".

The problem of "lack of mentorship" meant we promised "effective mentorship".

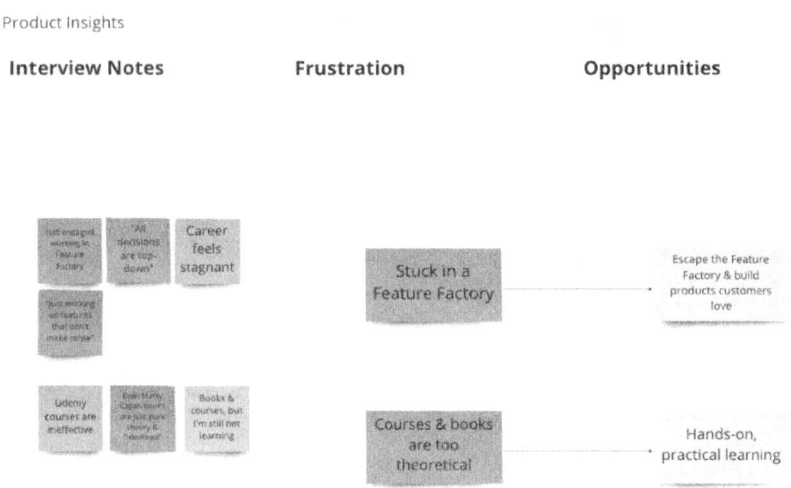

Finally, **it's important not to conflate opportunities with solutions.**

Opportunities are areas of value that we might want to deliver (e.g. more "speed"). We do not - at this stage - need to clarify exactly how we will deliver that value (e.g. will it be an email app, or a course, or a time-management tool?).

Many teams make the mistake of exploring a problem, then jumping into building the first solution they come up with.

This is wrong, as that solution is unlikely to have a clear product strategy - a clear unique insight driving it. Usually, this approach leads to launching a product that people just don't really care about, as it's not differentiated from the competition & doesn't really solve the right frustrations.

It's like rolling the dice in blackjack & blindly hoping for a win.

Instead, we want to be deliberate - & try to engineer success.

Rather than building random solutions, we want to only build solutions within a clear product strategy.

That starts with identifying the *right* opportunities.

How to Identify Opportunities to Inform Your Product Strategy?

Assuming you have done your discovery calls, the process of identifying opportunities is surprisingly simple.

There are 3 steps involved:

1. Identify common frustrations

First, we need to organise your discovery call notes.

Once you've conducted your ~10 discovery calls, despite following our lean approach to note-taking, you will have a lot of notes to sort through.

Perhaps an obvious, but important question to ask yourself: *Why are you taking notes in the first place?*

The goal with note-taking is to identify common trends across the different conversations we have had. That is easier when we visualise our insights.

Using our Prod MBA example, say we notice that our interviewee John complained that "courses & books are too theoretical", Sami mentioned that "he's read all the Marty Cagan books but doesn't know how to put it into action" & we observed that Jade seems fed up with paying for courses that only cover theoretical case studies?

| Udemy courses are ineffective | Even Marty Cagan books are just pure theory & "idealised" | Books & courses, but I'm still not learning |

In this case, we can identify a common frustration that connect John, Sami & Jade's frustrations:

"Current resources are too theoretical".

Once you've identified a shared frustration, you want to group those 3 related notes together, so that you can see who the frustration was relevant for (identifiable thorough colour-coding the notes) & what the exact quote or observation said.

Interview Notes	Frustration	Opportunities

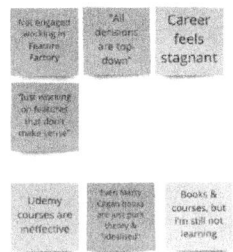

You should then read through all of your notes & write out 5-10 common frustrations that you have identified across your interviews. That may be a frustration that only came up once (if you felt it was a really acute frustration), or a frustration that came up multiple times.

You should end up with all the frustrations you've identified mapped out like so:

Product Insights

Interview Notes **Frustration** **Opportunities**

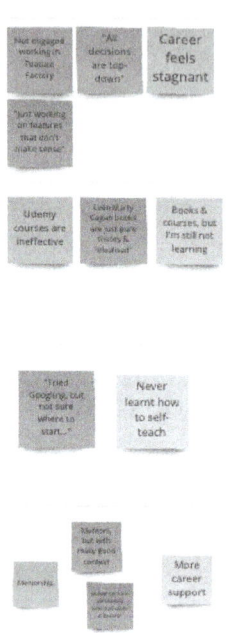

2. Prioritise Frustrations

Next, we want to prioritise the frustrations that we have identified.

To do so, you should go through your list of frustrations & identify which you feel are most acute. "Acuteness" is hard to quantify, however, so you can judge this based on number of times the frustration was mentioned (e.g. if mentioned by all of your interviewees, it's likely to be acute). You may, however, believe that a frustration that only one person mentioned was still super acute &

worth focusing on. And that is perfectly fine. How you define acuteness just depends on the unique problem space you are exploring.

Once you've identified what you feel are the 2-3 most acute frustrations, **highlight those frustrations by changing the colour of the card to red**.

(Note: This will not form your final list of opportunities. Once we do some competitive analysis in the next chapter, you may decide to focus on a different frustration entirely, or reduce the number of acute frustrations you might want to address. Therefore don't over-think this step.)

Interview Notes   Frustration   Opportunities

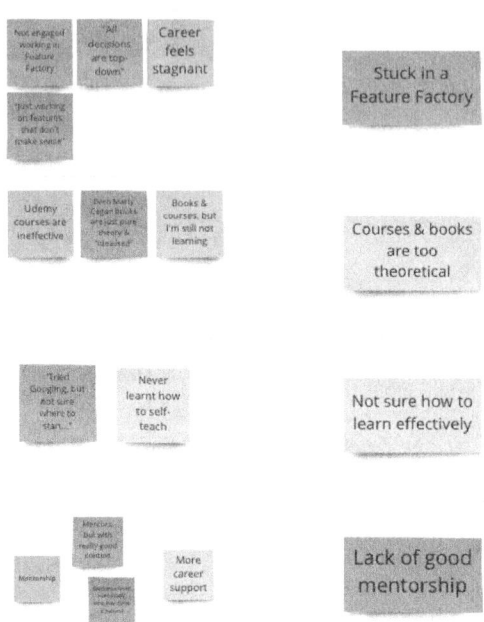

3. Flip Frustrations Into Opportunities

Finally, once you have a list of common, prioritised frustrations, you want to flip these to opportunities (i.e. where you see an area of value for your target customer).

If our users complain that email takes "2 hours per day", we might flip that to the opportunity of providing "lightning-fast email".

Returning to the Prod MBA example, if our frustration is "current resources are too theoretical", we might flip that to an opportunity of "hands-on & actionable learning", like so:

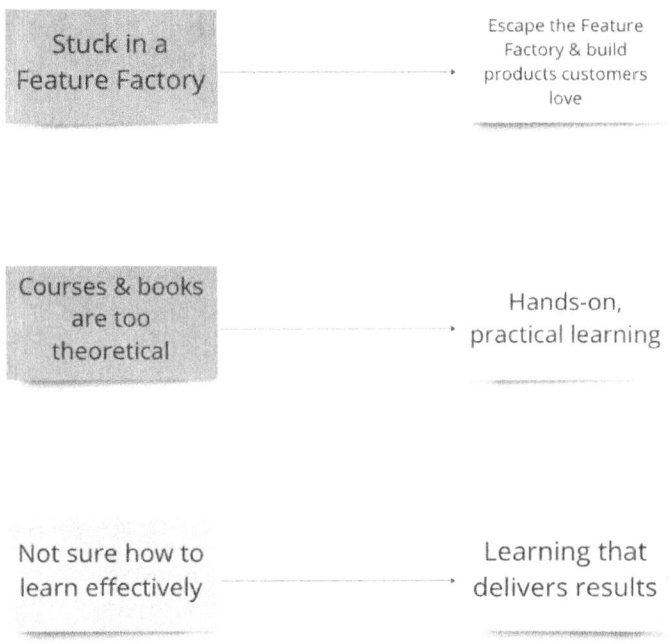

Go through all of your frustrations & write out the corresponding opportunity you have identified.

-

You should by now have identified your frustrations, prioritised what you feel are the most acute frustrations, then flipped these into concrete opportunities.

From this, you may already have uncovered one or more unique insights that you feel could drive your eventual product strategy (for example, a focus on "speed", like Superhuman).

However, before you move onto actually crafting our product strategy, you have one final step to complete:

Do some competitive analysis to understand whether you will, in fact, offer something that is genuinely *unique* in the market.

Putting This Into Practice

You've now identified the problem you want to solve, who you are solving it for, as well as uncovered some unique insights that could drive your product strategy.

Let's now craft a rough draft of your product strategy.

(You'll come back to improve this in the next chapter, once you've done our competitor analysis, but it's helpful to have a rough idea of where you think you will focus your product strategy already.)

In one sentence, *who* are you solving the problem for, what *ideal outcome* are you delivering for them & how might you solve that problem *in a unique way*?

To do so, you can use the following template: "We help [add niche] to [achieve ideal outcome] through [unique way you might deliver value]"

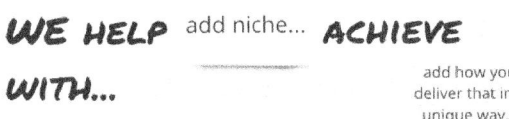

Example: "We help **young, London-based professionals** achieve **financial freedom by 30** through **automated inflation-proof investments**"

Download our Miro template here in order to put this into practice with your team.

How to Craft Your Product Strategy: Escaping The Competition

> "All failed companies are the same: they failed to escape competition." — Peter Thiel, Founder of Paypal & Palantir

A few years ago, I was working with a company that provided project management software.

They had a paying user base, consisting of corporate companies using it for their own teams, but were struggling to grow.

"*How can we get more users? And get them to stick around?*", they asked me.

"*Currently, you can't*", I responded bluntly.

Why?

Lack of differentiation.

I.E. they did not do anything different from anyone else in the market.

If you looked at their website, they just promised "project management software" & highlighted how they have all these features - features which their competition also had.

A solid, functional product, but so what?

There were another 10 products out there doing the same thing - doing it better in many cases!

Their strategy was to simply try & achieve feature parity with some of those competitors.

Now, you could say, "*well, the real reason for failure seems to be a lack of innovation*".

And you would be right.

But that lack of innovation to a large extent stems from a lack of understanding about product strategy.

This team, for example, was keen to innovate. They had even *paid me* to help them innovate! They just didn't understand how.

They felt they were innovating to an extent, because their roadmap wasn't fixed, so they considered themselves "agile". They were building something new (at least to them).

The problem was that that roadmap was coming from somebody else! From their competition. They were copying & trying always to play catch up, rather than focusing objectively - from first principles - on what their customers really wanted.

And it all came back to the same problem:

How could they come up with a unique product? One that was genuinely different from the competition?

So I told them, *"We need to discover a Blue Ocean."*

What is a Blue Ocean?

A Blue Ocean is a metaphor for finding a space in the market where there is little - or zero - competition.

It's a space where we can *find* users, *retain* them & *charge them a lot of money* for our product because of the fact that we are delivering a *unique set of value to them* that no other company is doing.

It's the Holy Grail for any product.

Google is a company that has operated in a Blue Ocean, for example, making huge profits because of their effective monopoly on Google Search & the advertising revenue that comes with it.

(Image credits[4])

In contrast, a Red Ocean - where my client found themselves - is where competition is fierce. It's where there are too many sharks in the water, all fighting for the same users & revenue.

It's the space where we *struggle to attract* users because we don't offer anything unique for them, *struggle to retain* them because our competition is always tempting them away, *struggle to charge* a lot of money for our product because a competitor is always trying to under-cut our prices.

---

[4] *Blue Oceans vs Red Oceans: What's the Right Strategy For Your Business?*, Tudor Dumitrescu

Surprisingly, a good example of operating in a Red Ocean is Uber.

Uber has failed to escape the competition.

It still haemorrhages money (it lost $8.5 BILLION in 2018 alone) because in every local market they compete in, competitors with lots of funding appear offering the same kind of service, at a lower price, with all sorts of sign-up bonuses to tempt users away from Uber.

Why is Finding A Blue Ocean So Important?

Quite simply, because lack of differentiation is the single biggest cause of product failure.

The best evidence we have is a study of reasons for startup failure:

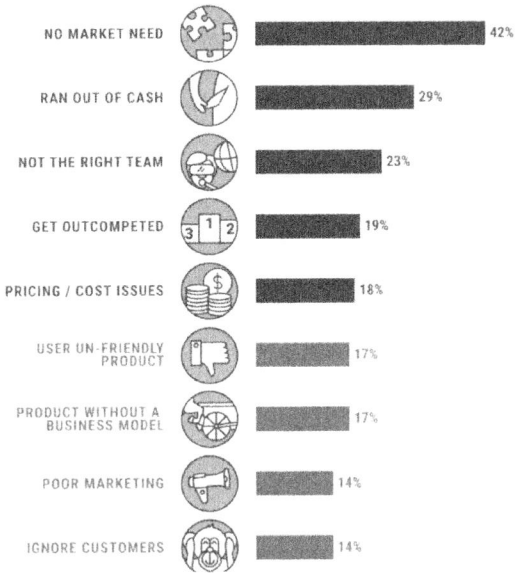

Of the top 9 reasons for startup failure[5], 6/9 of these can be attrributed to a lack of differentiation:

1. **No market need:** This is caused by not solving an acute problem, or when your solution already exists
2. **Ran out of cash:** A differentiated product should be able to charge more money to more customers because competition is less fierce
3. **Get outcompeted:** When another product does the same thing, but better
4. **Pricing:** An undifferentiated offer will always be in a price war (think of the amount of similarly priced olive oils on a supermarket shelf), which will make it difficult to become profitable

---

[5] Source: CBInsights study on startup failure rate

5. **Poor marketing:** If your message is not unique and compelling(i.e. they've seen it before), you'll struggle to acquire new users
6. **Ignore customers:** Not exploring the right opportunities, nor packaging these into a great product strategy

How to Find A Blue Ocean?

To find a Blue Ocean - that space without competition - we must attempt to offer something that:

1. Is **unique** (i.e. genuinely different from what already exists)
2. Is **valuable** (i.e. something that solves our niche's problem in a way that they find compelling & genuinely useful)

Both elements are essential. Why? As Peter Thiel, founder of Paypal, suggests, product teams should ask themselves:

"Is this intersection valuable?"

I.E. Are we actually providing something unique *and* valuable?

We could come up with some clever, unique solution. For example, a new career coaching product driven by AI. However, if that clever new solution doesn't actually deliver value, it will fail. And it's just different for the sake of being different.

In order to ensure you are offering something both unique *and* valuable, you must complete the [Blue Ocean Strategy Canvas][6]. This canvas is a framework we use to strategically differentiate ourselves from the competition.

The canvas consists of the following steps:

1. **Identify 4-5 existing alternatives currently in the market**
2. **Plot 5-10 areas of value that we and/or they offer our target customer**
3. **Rate how much value (from 0 to 10) each existing alternative for each area of value**
4. **Rate how much value (from 0 to 10) you aim to deliver on each area of value**
5. **Identify 1-3 areas of Blue Ocean**

Let's now go through each step in more detail.

Click here to access our digital Blue Ocean template.

---

[6] Developed by Renée Mauborgne and W. Chan Kim

Step 1/5: Identify 4-5 existing alternatives currently in the market

The first thing you want to do is identify your competition.

Competition can consist of **direct competitors**, but also what we call "**existing alternatives**" (essentially, any other way that the target customer currently solves the problem).

Imagine, for example, that we plan to launch a new project management tool to help Product Managers organise their work. We have obvious direct competitors, such as **Jira** or **Trello**. But we also have less obvious existing alternatives. Some Product Managers may use things like **Google Sheets**, or even a **personal to-do list**, or use **meetings**, to achieve the same goal (that of organising their work).

Remember: **Anything that your target customers uses to solve the problem is competition**.

Once you have identified your existing alternatives, you can add them to your template, like so:

Step 2/5: Plot 5-10 areas of value that you and/or those existing alternatives offer your target customer

Before plotting anything, what do we mean by "area of value"?

An area of value is not a feature or solution. When we talk about an "area of value", we are referring to a specific piece of value that can be delivered to our target customer. Thinking back to our Superhuman example, one such area of value would be "speed". For Prod MBA, another factor would be "hands-on learning".

It is essential that you do not, at this stage, try to compare features. **Features are quite simply a way - a vehicle - of delivering specific value to a target customer.** They are only as important as the value they deliver. And at this stage, we don't know - nor do we need to know - how specifically we will deliver value. We must, instead, focus on finding the unique value required to give us any chance of success. A unique value that will be packaged into our unique product strategy in the following chapters.

So remember: **Focus on value, not on features.**

(This is not to say we ignore features or solutions. In Superhuman's case, for example, the solution was relatively fixed (something related to "email"). We just want to stay open to different ways we might solve the problem.)

To identify which areas of value you could add to the canvas, you can do two things:

First, add the opportunities you have identified from your discovery calls.

Remember, the kind of competitive analysis the Blue Ocean provides should only be done **AFTER** you have spoken to your target customer so that you can come up with unique insights objectively, without getting distracted by the competition.

Using the Prod MBA example from the previous section, we could add the opportunities of "providing hands-on learning" and "effective mentorship" as two areas of value to deliver on.

Second, you can identify other areas of value that your existing alternatives provide by simply scanning their homepage and/or testing out the product.

What, for example, are they ultimately promising? Do they mention specific features? If so, what value are those features meant to provide? What value is mentioned in the testimonials? Does the product actually deliver on these areas of value when you test it out? Are there any other areas of value you can identify from testing the product out?

For example, imagine we have identified Trello as an existing alternative and we want to identify some areas of value Trello provides. On the homepage, we immediately see the promise that "Trello brings all your tasks, teammates, and tools together". From this we might identify "Aggregation of work" as an area of value. From testing Trello out, we might also feel that "collaboration" & "speed of task management" are things they do well.

From our discovery work, plus assessing our existing alternatives, we should come out with a list of 5-10 key areas of value. We then simply need to add these on the x-axis of our canvas like so:

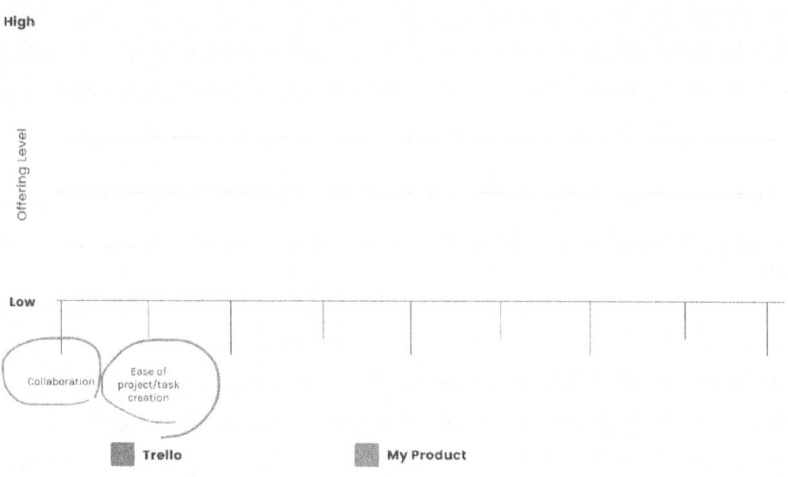

Step 3/5: Rate how much value (from 0 to 10) each existing alternative provides for each area of value

Next, you want to assess how well each existing alternative scores on each area of value.

From studying their homepage, reading reviews & testing out the product, you should have a sense of how well each product delivers a piece of value (e.g. On "collaboration", how would you rate Trello from 0 to 10?)

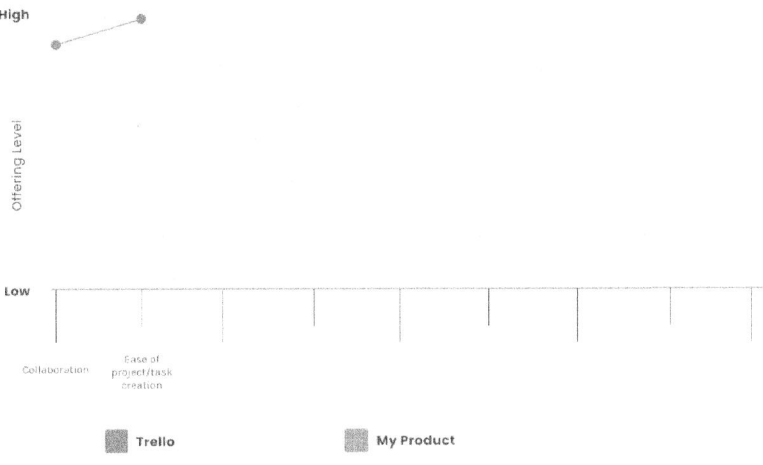

Providing a score from 0-10 is not an exact science. And you should not get too caught up on this (worrying whether you should rate Trello as a 6/10 or 7/10 for "collaboration", for example).

The key is that the scores are *comparative*. The key is that you have thought about how Trello rates on "collaboration" *compared to* another existing alternative, such as Google Sheets.

This is so you come out having plotted how each existing alternative scores on each area of value. This provides you with a clear, visual hierarchy of which product is better or worse in each area.

Once completed, your Blue Ocean Strategy Canvas should look like this:

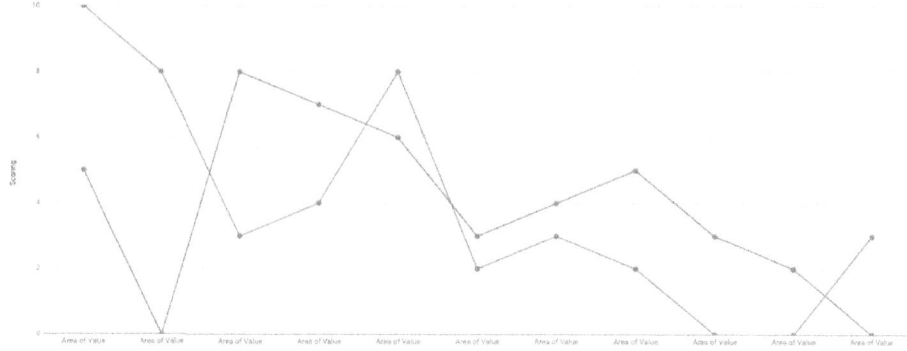

Step 4/5: Rate how much value (from 0 to 10) you aim to deliver on each area of value

The next step is to plot your own product's score.

Whether you are developing a new product, or auditing an existing product, this should be a *hypothetical* score i.e. what we want to achieve with your product.

You should therefore be aspirational, but also score your product on how much value you should deliver within a realistic timeframe (within the next 2 years is a good rough figure).

To score your product, use the insights gained from your product discovery calls:

Where, for example, did you see the most acute frustrations? And what did your interviewees suggest the competition was failing to do? How might you deliver the same value, but far better? Or provide the kind value that no one else is offering?

Furthermore, you should be aspirational, but also realistic. You will not, for example, be able to be good at everything. You shouldn't try to have the highest score on every single factor. In fact, you don't *want* to score highly on everything! Instead, you want to pick your battles & be really focused.

Take our project management example. There are many products out there. There are many great products out there, in fact.

It would be difficult to be more "collaborative" or "faster" than Trello. Or to give a more "detailed overview of work" than Jira. In this case, we might make the strategic decision to not even try to compete on these factors, but focus on something that they do badly, or don't do at all.

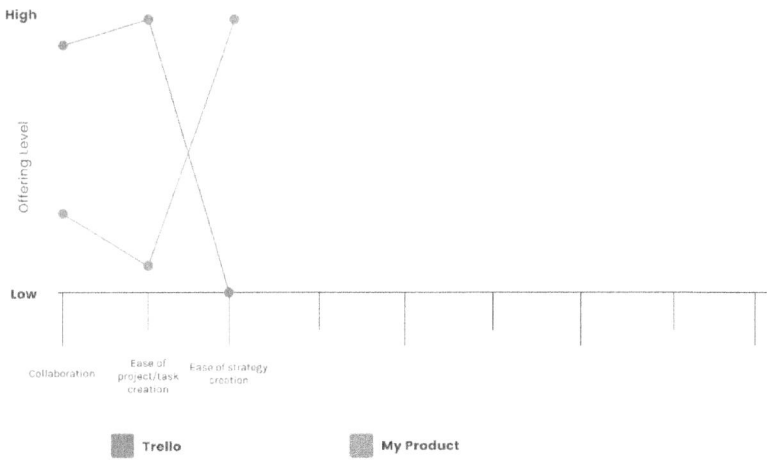

Step 5/5 Identify 1-3 areas of "Blue Ocean"

Once you have plotted the value you would like to deliver, as well as what your existing alternatives currently deliver, you should already have a rough idea of where you might focus your product strategy.

Example:

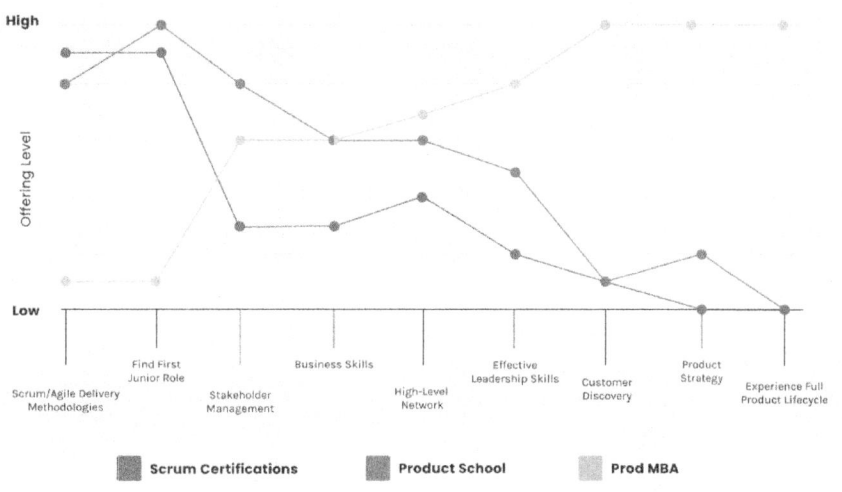

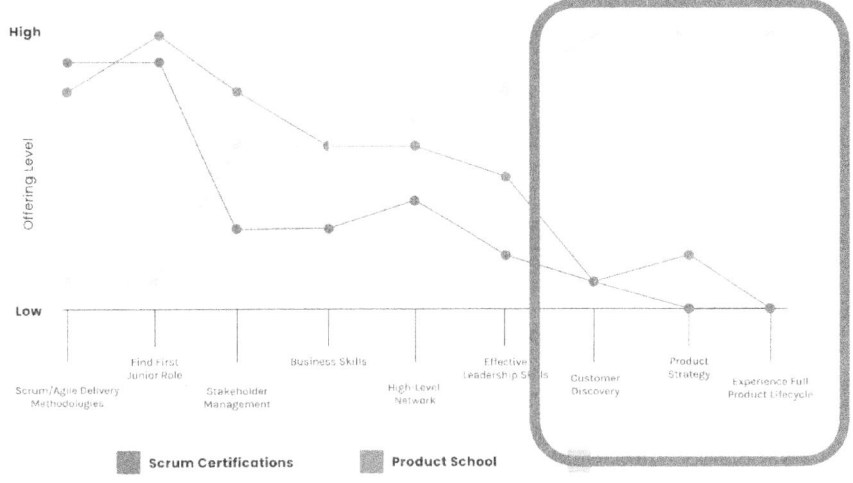

To help you decide what to focus on, however, you can use the Eliminate-Reduce-Raise-Create (ERRC) model[7]. This model helps us further improve our differentiation by asking the following questions of the factors we have on our Blue Ocean:

1. **Eliminate**: Which factors that the industry has long competed on should be eliminated?
2. **Reduce**: Which factors should be reduced well below the industry's standard? i.e. don't really matter
3. **Raise**: Which factors should be raised well above the industry's standard? i.e. under-valued
4. **Create**: Which factors should be created that the industry has never offered? i.e. unique value

---

[7] ELIMINATE-REDUCE-RAISE-CREATE (ERRC) GRID, Blue Ocean Strategy

To apply the ERRC model, you want to adjust the scores you gave your product, so that you:

1. Score *very low* (Eliminate) on roughly 25% of your areas of value
2. Score *quite low* (Reduce) on another 25%
3. Score *quite high* (Raise) on another 25%
4. Score *very high* (Create) on another 25%

Why? This will help you focus on the few areas of value that really matters as well as on new, unique areas of value that you can create for your target market.

Here's an example of ERRC in practice:

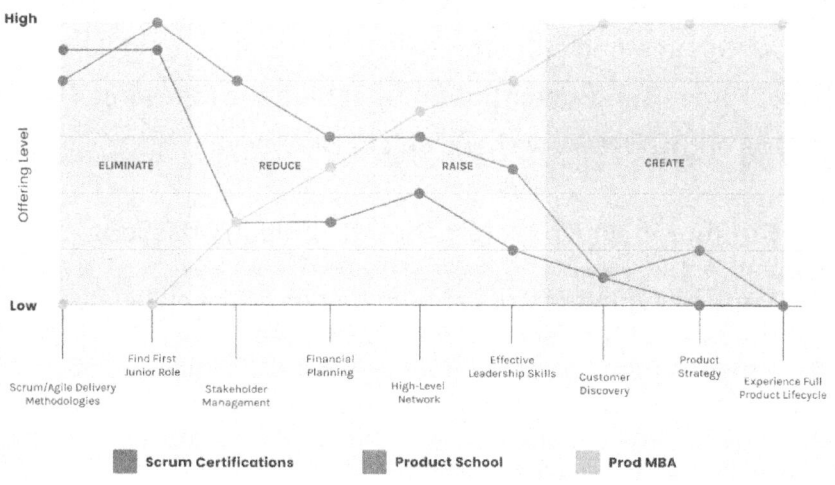

Conclusion

As Steve Jobs famously said,

> "Innovation is not about saying yes to everything. It's about saying no to all but the most crucial features."

The goal of applying the Blue Ocean Strategy Canvas, layered with the ERRC model, is to come out with a clear understanding of where you can offer something **both unique & valuable** to your target customer.

The next step?

Before you craft your final product strategy statement, it's essential to understand the different strategies underpinning a *winning* product strategy.

Putting This Into Practice

You should now have a very clear idea of which specific areas of value your product strategy could focus on.

Let's now improve the product strategy you drafted in the previous chapter:

Again, in one sentence, who are you solving the problem for, what ideal outcome are you delivering for them & how might you solve that problem in a unique way?

WE HELP add niche... **ACHIEVE** add their ideal outcome... **WITH...** add how you deliver that in a unique way...

Example: "We help **young, London-based professionals** achieve **financial freedom by 30** through **automated inflation-proof investments**"

Download our Miro template here in order to put this into practice with your team.

How To Craft A Winning Product Strategy: 3 Ways to Uncover Unique Value

In the last chapter, we looked at how you can methodically identify unique value in your market.

But to just say, "*come up with something unique & valuable to offer your niche*" isn't going to help you **actually** do that in reality.

In this chapter, we'll look at 3 different tactics you can apply to help uncover unique value, as well as specific examples for each:

1. Questioning convention
2. Using innovative technology
3. Focusing on doing one thing much better

To help us apply each tactic, let's use the following case study (a case study we asked Prod MBA students to solve in a live workshop).

Imagine you are tasked with exploring the following problem:

"Onboarding new employees is chaotic."

Hopefully, you now immediately then ask yourself a question:

What's the root problem? Why is "chaotic employee onboarding" a problem?

You might then think,

"Well, this is a problem because chaotic onboarding would mean a) it takes new employees **longer to create value** and b) they are **more likely to leave** if they aren't able to deliver value, buy into the company vision, get enough context about the businesses, etc. This is bad for any business."

You hopefully then ask yourself another question:

For *whom* is this problem most acute?

Rather than just "all employees" or "all companies", you might say,

"Well, why don't we focus in on growth-stage startups. It's likely more acute for them, as they suddenly start hiring rapidly with little hiring experience. It's super important their new hires are able to have impact, or the startup will fail."

Once we have a robust foundation, formed of the right problem to solve & a clear niche, we need to answer the key question:

How do we solve this problem *differently*?

Before we speak to our niche, or plot our Blue Ocean Strategy Canvas, however, it's useful to have some idea of how to "think differently" & come up with a genuinely unique, genuinely valuable product offer.

Here are 3 questions you can ask yourself:

1. How might you question convention?

When we started Prod MBA, I spoke to 30+ product professionals to understand how they were trying to accelerate their career progress.

One common theme, as I've highlighted before, was that "books & courses were too theoretical".

Why did this theme keep coming up, when there is so much literature showing that learning is simply not effective when based purely on consumption of content (e.g. passively watching some videos)?

Because of convention.

Specifically, two conventions:

a) The convention that education products (e.g. books, courses) should simply provide *theory* to a student & the student should then *work out how to apply it themselves*.

b) The convention that a company should always focus on scaling, meaning few companies provide the personalised support required to help reinforce any learning (i.e. they want to automate most everything & maximise profit, rather than student contact time).

In contrast, we realised that, for somebody to learn effectively, they need mentorship to adapt the theory to their unique context, they need motivation to actually bother applying it, accountability to apply & re-apply it, peers to learn from, etc.

They need more than just some videos to watch or pages to read!

So we questioned these conventions, asking ourselves,

"Why? Why can we not do things differently? And provide much more value in the process? And how might we give students a really hands-on, real-world learning experience?"

Our answer? By getting them to build a real product - teaching them the theory of product management & leadership in the process.

Other examples:

There was no "video doorbell" category before Ring.

There was no "hobbyist drone" category before DJI.

The idea of "ride-sharing" didn't exist before Uber.

All three questioned convention.

-

Returning to our employee onboarding problem, **how might you question convention in this context? What conventions exist?**

Do they make sense? And how might we approach things differently?

To start, you can list out 5-8 conventions that exist in this market. That could be behaviours and/or beliefs the niche has, or conventions that the competition follows.

From that list, you might realise that, for example, most companies follow a convention of getting their HR teams to manage the onboarding process.

Considering most of what an employee does is very specific to their role & domain (e.g. a Product Manager managing the payments product), you might decide this doesn't make sense. Why? Because HR don't really know much about that specific product, nor about product management generally. Therefore, you could re-think the onboarding process to be designed by those with the *right* domain & role expertise - the hiring manager, for example.

By doing so, you will have questioned a convention you believe doesn't make sense, and come up with a unique area of value to focus on in the process (i.e. empower the hiring manager to own onboarding, not HR).

2. How might you leverage new technologies?

When Tesla first started out, they didn't really have more than an idea to attempt to use lithium batteries to power electric cars.

In July of 2004, it built its first working prototype; the engineering team took the body of a Lotus Elise and fitted it with an AC propulsion drivetrain and prototype battery pack. The vehicle was dubbed Mule 1.

Through a lot of hard work by a lot of smart people, they have ended up today with a series of electric cars that are faster, more desirable, more efficient, than even most petrol cars.

Why? Because they leveraged a new technology (lithium batteries) at the moment the technology matured (i.e. those batteries could power a car for a long enough distance that owning one became feasible) & applied it very effectively to build a desirable product.

However, you don't always need to *invent* (or dramatically improve upon) a new technology to drive innovation.

Other companies see a new technology develop & *leverage it* to create a "paradigm shift" in a new market.

Loom, for example, is a product that allows you to rapidly record videos to share with your team.

Firstly, they questioned convention. Loom's team realised that most teams still communicated by email or comms platforms like Slack or Microsoft teams (i.e. by text). They realised this was slow & inefficient. They realised that communication by video would be faster & more efficient.

Secondly, they leveraged new technology. They were only able to question convention because the technology for recording videos online & storing those videos on the cloud had become fast enough - & data storage cheap enough - to make it a viable solution to offer.

Thirdly, they have since improved upon new advances in video & data storage to continue offering a faster, better video communication experience (and continue to do so with great success).

Returning to our employee onboarding problem, how might you leverage new technology?

You could, for example, focus on building an onboarding solution focused on "integration with workflow", integrating with the company's communication tools, calendar, project management tools, etc., to remove as much friction as possible from the onboarding experience, as just one example.

3. How might you do one thing much better?

In 1999, Nick Swinmurn had an idea:

Selling shoes online.

The problem?

No investor wanted to go near him!

The low margins, the difficulties of finding the right size, customers returning models they didn't like, etc., just made it an unattractive business proposition.

Yet Nick did manage to convince some investors to fund the business.

And that business was called Zappos.

10 years later, Zappos was bought by Amazon for $1.2 billion.

How? They focused on doing one thing way better than any of their competitors: Customer service.

They didn't just want to help their customers when, for example, the customer opened the customer support chat. They wanted to **wow** *each & every customer,* going so far as to put *every single* new employee - whatever the role - through a 4-week training programme when joining, in order to provide the best customer support possible.

Zappos was hugely successful because they didn't focus on providing the most shoe varieties, or exclusive models, or the lowest prices. They focused on doing one single thing much better than everybody else: the customer experience.

And you can follow the same approach for your own product strategy:

Identify one area of value that you can deliver 10x better than the competition on.

A few examples for inspiration:

- **Simplicity**: whereby.com, for example, allows you to start a video call by simply clicking a URL (no sign up or clicking boxes asking for permission to access camera, video, etc.)
- **Speed**: Superhuman, for example, focuses on helping you save hours each day with a "lightning fast" email service
- **Delight**: SW Airlines, for example, aims to delight every single customer with anything from fun security announcements to truly human customer interactions
- **Leveraging network**: Google Search, for example, focused on improving its core product through more people using the product, thus improving the search algorithm (more on this in the next chapter)
- **Professional-looking photos**: Instagram, for example, focused on the seemingly unimportant insight that many users wanted to create & share professional-looking photos. They added "filters" & saw usage take off, helping them become the dominant player in their market

Whether it's focusing on speed, customer delight or anything else of value, focusing on doing one thing really effectively is always a smart strategy.

Conclusion

By asking these 3 questions, you start to frame how you think about where unique value might lie for your product. By doing so, you can dramatically improve our product strategy.

However, always remember: "thinking differently" & coming up with a unique way to solve a problem rarely comes from sitting in a conference room with your team, or spending hours preparing an Excel spreadsheet.

Unique insight comes from speaking to your target customer, really getting to know them - and backing that up with the kind of exercises we've outlined in the last few chapters to help you generate different ideas (one of which will hopefully form the core of your winning product strategy.)

Putting This Into Practice

So far, you should have a draft of your product strategy:

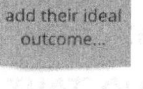

Now you can try to improve it further by asking yourself the follow questions:

1. **How might you question convention?**
2. **How might you leverage new technologies?**
3. **How might you do one thing much better?**

Here's an example from Miro, the collaborative tool, using our Miro template:

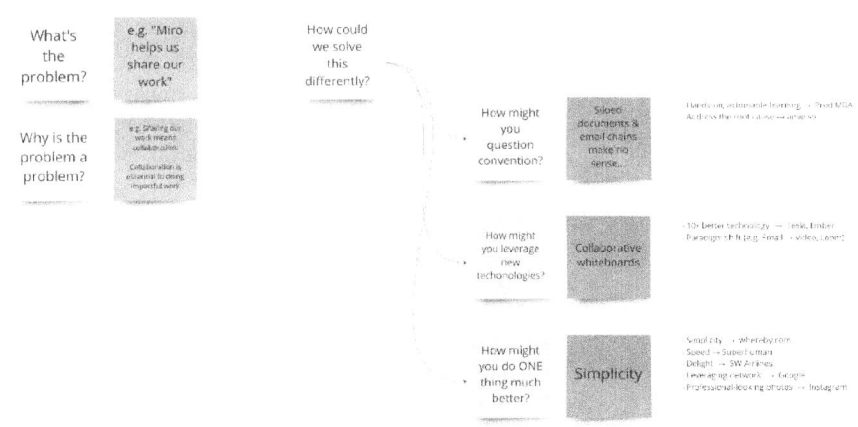

For each question, simply write down 4-5 different ideas.

Remember that quality comes from quantity, so the more ideas you get down, the better.

Once you've generated some ideas, go back to your product strategy first draft & see whether you would change the final part ("how you deliver value in a unique way").

How To Craft A Winning Product Strategy: Strategies for Long-Term Dominance

You now have the ingredients for a great product strategy: An acute problem to solve, a clear target market & a unique way we can deliver value.

However, product success can be short-lived.

We could, for example, launch or relaunch our product around a really effective product strategy of being the "most frictionless" video call product ever. We might get some really strong early success, with happy repeat users - even paying customers!

Yet that success might draw the attention of Zoom or Slack or Microsoft Teams. With far more resources & huge existing user bases, they can simply copy what we do, use the loyalty of their existing customer base, and gradually take our market share until we run out of money & fail.

You therefore want to ask yourself one final question before you craft your final, winning product strategy:

How might you create & maintain dominance in the long-term?

By asking this question, you will likely draw one of two possible conclusions:

1. We do not need to change our product strategy

Take Zappos, for example. They believed that people would continue to buy shoes for the foreseeable future. They also realised that shoes were inherently tricky. There's no one-size-fits-all, meaning there will always be a certain level of returned items & customer support interactions.

Therefore remaining laser focused on providing exceptional "customer support" would make sense now & it would make sense for the foreseeable future.

2. We need to evolve our product strategy over time

Take Slack, for example. Slack has grown extremely quickly because they make it *frictionless* & *fast* to communicate with your team.

However, their market dominance is being gradually eroded by Microsoft Teams. Because many organisations pay for Microsoft software already (e.g. Word, Excel), they understandably use/switch to the Teams product, as it's included in that software package.

Slack is therefore, as of 2022, looking at ways to solve more than just the problem of "instant communication", with features like file sharing, integration with your workflow & much more, in order to out-compete Microsoft.

They have therefore *evolved* their product strategy over time.

3. We need to change our product strategy *immediately*

Once you understand the different tactics you can use to achieve long-term market dominance, you may want to change your product strategy.

Remember: The goal is to come out with the best product strategy possible. To come up with a *winning* product strategy: One you believe will help you acquire, retain & charge your users effectively, as well as one that will allow you to maintain that market share *over the long-term.*

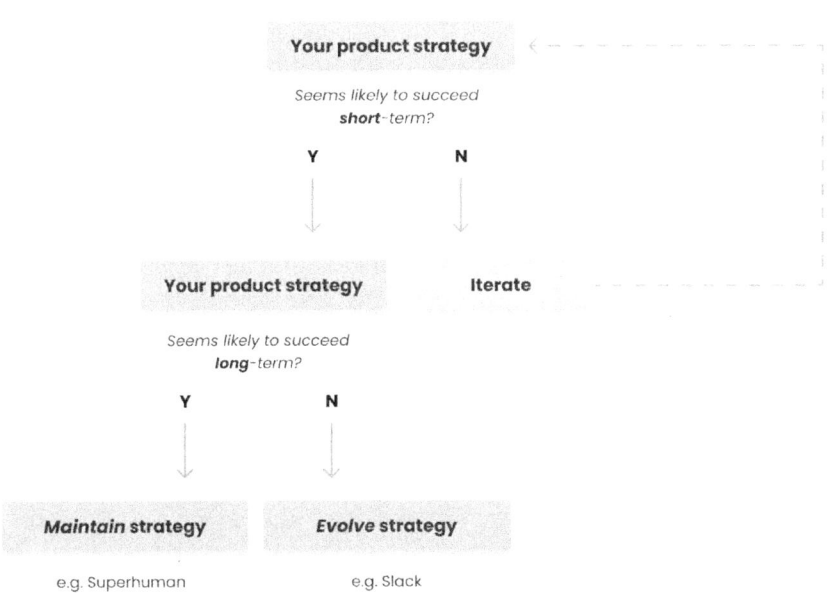

In the next section, we'll look at 3 specific tactics you could apply to improve your product strategy.

How to Maintain Long-Term Dominance: 3 Tactics Used By Hugely Successful Businesses

1/3 Network Effects

A network effect is where a product gains additional value the more people use it.

Take Google Search, for example. Google Search initially wasn't very good!

It had some ability to find content for you based on simple search terms. If you searched for "Chocolate cake recipe", it would show you any webpages with those key words. But a more nuanced search? Such as "best way to craft a product strategy" would struggle to surface the best articles on the subject.

Over time, however, Google Search has improved dramatically for its end users.

Why?

Because, the more you & other people search, the better Google's algorithm gets at interpreting your searches & finding relevant content (if, for example, you spend a lot of time on a certain page, it can determine that that page likely has valuable content on it, so it will push it up the rankings).

This creates more value for you as the end user, but also more value for Google as a business. Why? The richer the data Google has on each user, the more valuable that is for advertising, who can better target you with relevant adverts.

Furthermore, most networks are inherently *social*.

Social media platforms like Tiktok or Instagram grew so rapidly because the more your friends are on the platform, the more valuable the platform is for you. Therefore, there was a big incentive to invite your friends to the platform in order to interact with them. This word-of-mouth referral mechanism drove acquisition far more effectively than any paid advertising campaign could.

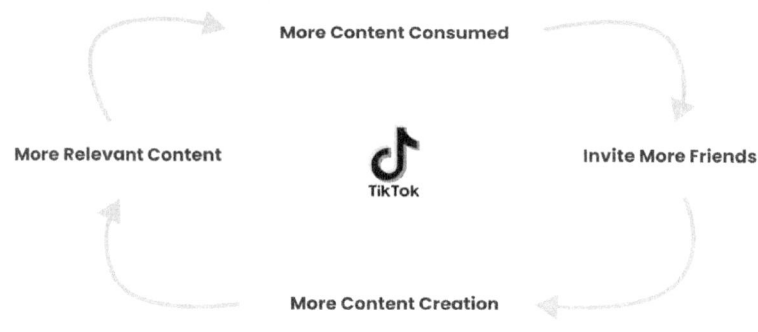

If you are able to leverage network effects, it can be extremely powerful.

The more users you gain, the more valuable the product gets for those users. The more valuable the product gets for those users, the more value you can capture in the form of revenue.

Network effects become a virtuous cycle of growth that make it extremely difficult for your competitors to copy effectively - what we call a "defensible moat" around your product.

Specifically, we can try to leverage network effects by following the following tips & tactics:

The more users, the better the product gets:

This is the general approach outlined above, Google Search being a great example of this in practice.

Leveraging referral:

You can try to incentivise your users to invite others to the platform in order to drive organic referral. Rather than adding something outside of your core value (such as a separate referral programme), you can in many cases bake referral into your core product experience.

Loom is an excellent example of this.

The core functionality is not just *recording videos* to capture some sort of important content. It is also to *share* that with whoever needs to consume that content. By sharing the video link, you are sharing Loom with those external users, many of whom will then sign up for Loom themselves if they see enough value in the product.

Avoid clustered networks:

If you try to leverage network effects, it's best to focus on networks whose value go beyond fixed geographical or digital boundaries.

Uber, for example, is used across the globe. However, there's one big problem with their business model: They have clustered networks.

It doesn't matter to me, sitting in London, that Uber is used in Sydney & New York. It just matters whether I can find a driver near me that will get me from A to B quickly & cheaply. The clustered network is therefore based around *London* drivers & *London* users looking for a ride.

Uber is haemorrhaging billions of dollars each year because they are unable to dominate the ride share market: A new competitor will keep popping up in every city with an incentive to ride with them ("Free first ride!"), with competitive prices & ambitious investors willing to bankroll them until they carve out significant market share.

Free-Riding Off an Existing Network

Another clever tactic is to embed your product with an existing network.

Visa is a great example of this. For many payments across the world, Visa is there, quietly in the background, providing the technology to facilitate that payment.

Rather than trying to acquire Visa users & do everything in the payments space, they are happy to integrate with big banks, digital payment systems, payment machines, etc., to continue growing their market share.

Adding Value Through Data

Perhaps the most fashionable - but very effective - network effect can be the use of data that your product gathers over time in order to add further value.

Amazon's recommendations algorithm is a good example of leveraging data to add value in practice.

In the early days, there was no algorithm. Amazon would simply recommend other products based on your previous purchases or search terms. If, for example, you search for "romance novel", it might show other books with the tag "romance". Very simple, but still effective. And still leveraging your data to add value.

Over time, that recommendations algorithm became far more effective, both as the machine learning technology improved, and as Amazon gathered more historic data on each user.

Now, for many Amazon users, they have such rich data that they can suggest products you probably never even thought you needed!

(It's worth emphasising that, particularly in this case, our product strategy may have different sequential stages to it. We can't, for example, start with an amazing recommendations algorithm if we have no user data! We may, therefore, focus on providing an "unbeatable customer experience", whilst stacking value with "great recommendations" over time.)

2/3 Economies of Scale

As well as leveraging network effects, your business may benefit from economies of scale i.e. your costs getting lower the more products you sell.

This can be driven by greater negotiating power. For example, when we buy 100 iPhones from Apple to sell v. When we buy 1,000,000 iPhones from Apple to sell, we can negotiate a different price.

It can also be driven by improvements in distribution. Amazon, for example, is able to ship products extremely quickly because of automation & autonomous robots performing a majority of tasks in their distribution centres.

Usually it is large companies selling physical products benefit most from economies of scale, such as Amazon or Walmart.

3/3 Brand

Worth also mentioning is the power of brand in maintaining long-term dominance.

If we look objectively at a product created by a company like Cisco, Oracle or SAP, for example, those products could rightly be seen as slow & clunky.

However, many companies & individuals will still use - & purchase - those products because the Cisco brand is reliable. Who, for example, has ever been fired from a corporate company for using a Cisco or SAP product?

As opposed to taking the perceived *risk* of trying some new startup that might go out of business next year?

Putting Theory into Practice

It is therefore worth pausing to ask yourself:

Do you need to create a defensive moat that will protect your product long-term? And how might you leverage network effects, economies of scale and/or a strong brand to maintain dominance?

This might not be a change you make to your short-term product strategy, but a different step in your product strategy - an evolution - that you could pivot to once initial market share is gained (think Amazon & the recommendations algorithm which took years to build).

Again, go back to your product strategy draft & see whether you want to update anything:

How To Craft A Winning Product Strategy: The Minimal Viable Offer

When one of our students, Richard, graduated Prod MBA, he wanted to test out his new-found knowledge & confidence with his team.

Having just started a new role as Product Lead at a growing startup, it was the perfect opportunity to talk about product strategy:

The founders weren't really sure what their unique value was, and teams were building any feature idea that came up. In short, there was no product strategy.

So Richard got to work defining possible product strategies, validating those product strategies, and, finally, aligning the team around a shared product strategy that would direct all of their work.

This has helped them go on to build a hugely successful product, helping consumers get *fair compensation* for flight delays & cancellations.

Beyond that, it also helped Richard avoid all the usual in-fighting, confusion & conflicting interests that plague most product organisations within a matter of weeks.

But what did Richard do specifically to make this happen?

He used the MVO.

What is the MVO?

The MVO refers to the Minimal Viable Offer.

We define it as:

> "A statement outlining what value we will deliver to our audience & how we will deliver that value in a unique way."

In simple terms, it's a way of **defining & validating a unique value proposition before really building anything**.

It should outline:

- *Who* the product is for
- What *ideal outcome* it will deliver for those people
- How you will deliver that outcome *in a unique way*

You have, in fact, gradually been building your own MVO over the last few chapters. You should recognise the format:

We help [*niche*] achieve [*their ideal outcome*] by [*unique way you deliver that ideal outcome*]

e.g. **We help [*busy CEOs*] to [*save 2-3 hours per day*] with [*the fastest email experience ever*]**

Why Should You Use the MVO?

Remember what a product strategy is from previous chapters:

> "The product strategy describes how the long-term goal is attained; it includes the product's value proposition, market, key features, and business goals." — Strategize: Product

Strategy and Product Roadmap Practices for the Digital Age, Roman Pichler

The MVO represents our product strategy, outlining the core elements of that product strategy: the value proposition, market, even key features in some cases.

By packaging your product strategy into an MVO statement, you are therefore able to do the following 3 things:

1. Define your product strategy
2. Validate your product strategy
3. Communicate your product strategy

Implementing Product Strategy

1. Define your product strategy

The key part of any product strategy is the unique value proposition.

Unfortunately, traditional business teaching & Roman Pilcher's definition of product strategy tend to obfuscate - or at least play down - the importance of a unique value proposition.

Remember: **We live in a world with 10x the competition than 10 years ago[8]**. Furthermore, remember that 6/9 of the key reasons startups fail comes down to a lack of differentiation.

Consider also that 80% of products never achieve Product-Market Fit[9], as a product leader, it is therefore essential to *obsess* over discovering what you believe is a *genuinely unique* value proposition in order to lay the foundation for Product-Market Fit - & the growth that will help your products not just survive, but thrive.

Most MBAs or product books will say, "Just come up with a unique value proposition".

However, we know that, in the real world, it isn't that easy.

This is why you should be very explicit in defining your unique value proposition.

The MVO is the most effective way to do so.

2. Validate your product strategy

> "What the smartest companies know is that we have to earn the right to build." - Gigi Levy-Weiss

---

[8] Based on the number of websites, generally representing an individual product, from 2008-2018, Statista
[9] The New Mindset for Product-Market Fit, Gigi Levy-Weiss

A great product strategy ultimately is as much about what we do **not** focus on, as what we **do** focus on.

It comes down to being crystal clear about what unique value our product promises, and what unique value it needs to deliver (e.g. *speed* in the case of Superhuman); then, simply not worrying about everything that lies outside of that unique value proposition.

Melissa Perri, CEO of ProdUX, defines product strategy as follows:

> "A good strategy is not a plan; it's a framework that helps you make decisions… Strategy creation is the process of determining the direction of the company and developing the framework in which people make decisions."

If we are going to commit all of our resources to a product strategy, therefore, it's important that we know it is the right product strategy!

I.E. that what we are proposing to offer is considered unique *and* valuable by our niche.

Once we have defined the MVO, we can validate whether it is valuable before needing to build the actual solution. It means we must *"earn the right to build"* by validating that product strategy before we even think about a solution to help us deliver on that strategy.

You can, for example, write you MVO on a simple landing page that you send to prospective users. If they sign up for the offer, it suggests your offer is at least interesting (if not compelling). If not, it suggests you may not be offering something unique & valuable. Therefore, you may need to iterate.

This gives us a strong signal that the product strategy is correct - helping us answer some big, essential hypotheses around the value prop, the market, key features and business goals that product success will depend upon - before we commit to building any solution.

3. Communicate your product strategy

You could come up with the most clever, multi-stage product strategy in the world. **However, it won't matter if your stakeholders do not *commit* to it.**

It's not enough to simply define & validate a product strategy.

You must be able to *communicate* the product strategy in order to get stakeholders on board: To help them understand the product strategy, rally around that product strategy, as well as get them involved in shaping that product strategy.

Even more important, you need to communicate it in a way that is very simple and concrete - very memorable - so that those stakeholders remain focused on that product strategy.

Superhuman, for example, is not just successful because they came up with a compelling product strategy (being the "*fastest email service ever*"). They are so successful because they *remain* laser-focused on providing an even faster email service.

Superhuman's team is not distracted by shiny new things.

They focus on things that increase speed - and ignore everything else.

Communicating product strategy with your stakeholders so they not just understand it - but keep it top of mind when making decisions - is essential to product success. The MVO is the most effective way for helping you achieve this.

How to Craft Your MVO?

Crafting your MVO is surprisingly simple, as you have done most of the work already.

As stated above, we need to include the following:

- *Who* is the product for?
- What *ideal outcome* will it deliver for your niche?
- How will you deliver that outcome *in a unique way*?

We package that into the following template:

Example:

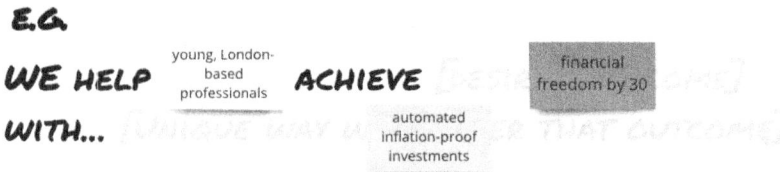

If you've successfully ignored the "Putting This Into Practice" sections up until this moment, now is the time to at least attempt your own product strategy using this template (which, by the way, is available in our Miro template).

1. Who is the product for?

At this stage, you should have identified the specific niche you will be focusing on.

For an early-stage product or one that has not achieved Product-Market Fit, this should be as specific a group as possible (e.g. CEO of a remote B2B startup). For mature, growing products, that may mean a broader group (e.g. all remote teams).

WE HELP add niche...

2. What ideal outcome should you deliver?

From exploring the problem & identifying opportunities in your product discovery work, you should also have identified what outcome your niche ultimately wants.

(Remember those acute frustrations you flipped into opportunities?)

You might want to review your notes & add it to your MVO template in as concise & compelling a way possible:

WE HELP add niche... **ACHIEVE**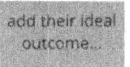

e.g. We fast-track **PMs** to **Head of Product**

This, by the way, actually constitutes the core of your product *vision* (an aspirational, ~5-year outcome your product will drive towards that can be used to inspire your team).

3. How will you deliver that outcome in a unique way?

Finally, you need to add that unique differentiator to your MVO statement so that your niche understands that you are solving this in a different, potentially much better way.

This, in turn, means they perceive it to be worth - at the very least - testing it out to see whether your unique product helps them move towards their desired outcome.

This essentially allows us to validate the crux of the MVO:

Is our proposed unique value actually something they seem to value? If so, it is worth us taking the next step to develop & test out a solution.

Once you have defined how you will deliver the niche's desired outcome in a truly unique way, add it to the MVO template:

WE HELP add niche... **ACHIEVE** add their ideal outcome... **WITH...** add how you deliver that in a unique way...

Here is another example:

Note: We have also created an MVO Calculator, a simple Google Sheets to help you experiment with different word combinations:

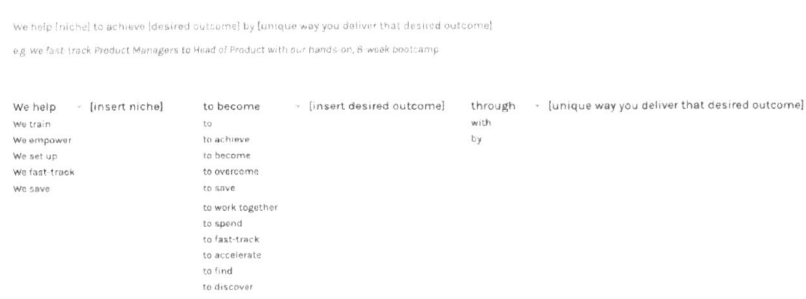

You can also adapt the MVO structure to suit your unique MVO. Just make sure you still include the key elements of your niche, their desired outcome & your unique approach to delivering that desired outcome.

Finally, many of you will be thinking:

What about the solution?! I have no idea what we would even build, so how can I come up with an MVO already?!

In some cases, the solution IS essential to the core value proposition, it's true. Like Superhuman, it might be a known problem (e.g. email taking up 2 hrs per day) that requires great execution on a pretty fixed solution (e.g. some sort of email tool).

However, in most cases, you do not even need to mention the solution. The thing your niche values is not a solution, but the **value** you will deliver them.

For Prod MBA, for example, Product Managers don't really care that we offer the solution of "an 8-week bootcamp". They care about the outcome we promise ("fast-tracked to Head of Product") & the unique way we deliver ("hands-on learning building a real product").

Do we deliver that with a bootcamp? With AI? With coaching?

It doesn't really matter.

The important thing to know is:

Does my niche care about the unique value of "hands-on learning" or "building a product from scratch"?

That's it.

It's as simple as adding those 3 elements together to be clear about what value we deliver before the next stage:

Validating your MVO.

How to Validate Your MVO?

Before we talk about how to validate your MVO, it's important to be clear about what we mean by "validation" & why this is such an important step.

Validating your MVO refers to **an attempt to see that your niche finds value in what you are proposing to offer them**.

That does not mean that you can prove that your target market will ultimately use - & pay for - the solution you end up building.

Instead, you are looking for signal from your niche; some indication that they are interested in testing out your product & potentially paying for it.

This signal could come in the form of the number of people who sign up for your Beta programme, or a B2B customer willing to make a pre-payment commitment for your product.

(We'll talk more about how we validate different products & measure success in more detail in the next section.)

Why is Getting Signal From Your Niche So Important?

It may seem an obvious point, but it's worth stating:

Committing to a product strategy means we are committing to focus on a specific area of value, building *only* products & features that help us deliver *that specific area* of value (e.g. more *speed*, in the case of Superhuman).

This means we are not focusing on many other things.

If, therefore, we are committing all of our resources to doing A (and not B, C, D, E, F, etc.), we want to be as confident as possible that A is in fact something our niche really values.

Not only something they value, but something they are willing to put some commitment into achieving.

This could be a *time* commitment of signing up to learn more, a commitment of *effort* by booking a call with us or trying the solution we end up developing; it could also be a *financial* commitment of actually paying for the product.

With one of these forms of commitment, you can be confident developing a solution that will help you deliver the unique value you promise your niche.

Furthermore, validation also helps us avoid many of the psychological biases that undermine product success.

Why?

Teams that jump straight into building a solution without a clear product strategy struggle to pivot when things are not going to plan. This is because they are more likely to stick with something when they have already sunk time & money into that solution (what we call the "sunk-cost bias"). Furthermore, they are more likely to manipulate data (consciously or not) in order to feel justified in continuing to pursue a certain solution (what we call "confirmation bias").

Add to that attentional bias (where by focusing on Solution A, we fail to consider Solution B/C/D/etc.), and it becomes a lot harder to pivot when following the wrong path once we have committed to a solution.

Validating your MVO therefore helps you be confident that you are able to provide unique value to the market, as well as avoiding the traps of doubling down on a solution that doesn't make sense.

How to Validate Your MVO?

How, though, do we actually validate an MVO in practice?

Ultimately, **there is no single way to do this**.

Validation will depend on the stage of your product, whether you have an existing audience, what your acquisition funnel looks like, whether you have a concrete idea of your solution, and more.

However, there are two concrete approaches we suggest following that I will outline below.

Early-Stage Products

If you are developing a completely new product from scratch, whether as a startup or in an existing organisation, then every element of how you validate your MVO must be built from scratch.

There are 4 stages to validating your MVO in this case:

1. Building your MVO funnel
2. Finding your niche
3. Attracting your niche to your MVO
4. Activating your niche

MVO Funnel: New Products

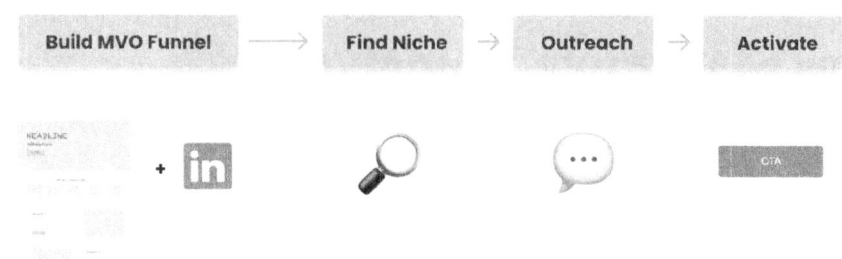

1/4 Building your MVO funnel

First, you will need to prepare a funnel in order to convert your niche in some way once you have found them & reached out to them.

That funnel consists of a very simple landing page.

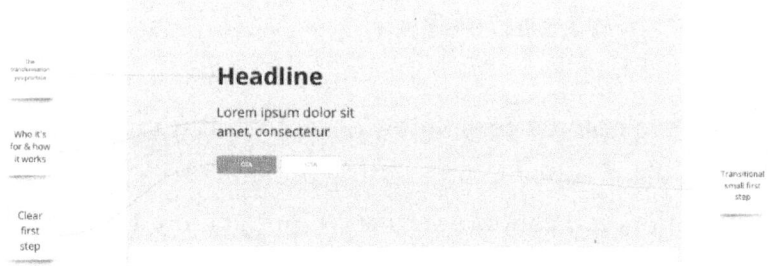

Your landing page should consist of the following elements

1. **Headline:** This should state your MVO
2. **Support text:** This can outline briefly what you do & why that is relevant for your niche (reinforcing the MVO)
3. **Email signup:** There should be a very clear call-to-action to clearly state what the next step is that your niche should

take if they are interested. We suggest a call-to-action stating that you have just launched a Beta programme & encouraging your niche to sign up to "Join The Waiting List"
4. **Main image**: This should reinforce the desired outcome you promise to deliver your niche. It is also optional, as the MVO is the most important element for attracting your niche, but you may find suitable, free stock images on unsplash.com

We teach students using Softr, a tool for building no-code landing pages & full products. However, it doesn't matter which platform you use to build your landing page, as long as you are able to collect emails from your website visitors.

Here's an example:

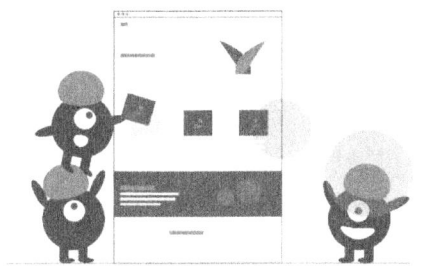

(As a bonus, you can also encourage those who have signed up to book a call with you, so you can gather more qualitative data through a discovery call. You can also encourage them to fill out a short survey, asking them a few questions to shed more light on the problem space (see example survey here))

2/4 Finding Your Niche

Once you have your basic MVO funnel setup, you need to identify where your niche hangs out.

You should already know where your niche hangs out from the discovery work you did in identifying your target niche, as actually being able to find them ("addressability") was a key component of defining your target niche.

The niche could be hanging out on online forums, LinkedIn, Facebook groups, following certain Instagram hashtags, at in-person meet-ups or more. If there is no obvious place to find your niche, try to think outside the box & explore different possibilities.

3/4 Attracting your niche to your MVO

Once you know where your niche hangs out, it's time to attract them to your MVO.

To do so, you first need to contact them directly in some way.

If you use LinkedIn, for example, you might search "Junior Product Manager" (your niche), then directly add 50 Junior Product Managers. A few days later, once some of those 50 people have accepted your invitation to connect, you can pitch your MVO in order to try & attract them to your landing page. We suggest using the following message template:

"Hi [first name], we help [niche] achieve [desired outcome] by [unique way we deliver that outcome]. We're launching a Beta programme that is completely free & think you would be a good fit. Are you interested in learning more?"

e.g. "Hi John, we help fast-track Product Managers to Head of Product by getting you to build a real product from scratch. We're launching a Beta programme that is completely free & think you would be a good fit. Are you interested in learning more?"

If they respond saying they are interested, you can then send them a link to your landing page.

If using LinkedIn, we suggest adding the link to your landing page to your About section in order to attract more leads. We also suggest adding the MVO in your headline so it's as visible as possible.

There are many tips & tactics for attracting your niche.

Some are platform-specific (you can add a headline to your LinkedIn profile, for example, but not on your Reddit profile). Others are relevant for all platforms (building trust over time by interacting with your niche on community forums, LinkedIn comments, etc., before reaching out to them).

The important thing is to understand the principles behind how to attract your niche:

Build trust with them in some way (usually through a credible profile & interacting with the niche before reaching out to them).

Next, **clearly state your MVO**, so they understand what is in it for them by interacting with you.

Finally, a **call-to-action** to visit your website to learn more so they clearly understand what the next step should be (if they are interested in learning more).

4/4 Activating your niche

Finally, once those interested are able to click through to your landing page, the landing page should do the work for you:

Reminding them of the MVO & clearly stating what they can do next: Adding their email to your waiting list.

Once they have signed up, you can consider them activated i.e. they have taken some concrete action to engage with your MVO, providing you with signal that your MVO is something they are at least curious about - if not very interested in trying out.

This is the kind of signal you need to give you confidence that you can now move on to thinking about which solutions to build.

So, through a simple landing page & campaign to reach out to people from your niche, you can rapidly validate whether your MVO seems to be something genuinely valuable; something worth committing your team's resources to.

Success

Finally, we are still stuck with one important question at this stage:

How do we measure success?

There's no definite way of quantifying success. After observing over 300 different MVO experiments with our students & other Product Managers, however, we suggest using the following *rough* benchmarks:

- If **50%** of those you have contacted sign up to your offer, then you probably have a *very* compelling MVO
- If **20-50%**, your MVO is likely compelling
- If **10-20%**, your MVO is at least interesting
- If **<10%**, your MVO should be iterated

Just be aware that these are *rough* benchmarks that are affected by *many* factors worth factoring into your decision to stick or iterate your MVO.

For example, does contacting people who already know you make them more likely sign up than a random person? Does the extra step in your LinkedIn outreach mean you'll get fewer views than, for example, Facebook outreach? Did you add visuals to your funnel? Is your LinkedIn profile optimised to help sell your MVO? Etc.

Existing Products

For existing products, you can use the MVO as a powerful tool to audit what your product offers by validating one of a few different MVOs in order to understand what we should focus on (e.g. is it "speed" or "customer experience"?).

The process for validating your MVO is more simple in this case, as you already have access to your audience (unless you are completely changing direction with your product & targeting an entirely new audience, in which case I suggest following the steps for early-stage products).

There are 3 steps:

1. Build your MVO survey
2. Get your niche to fill in your MVO survey
3. Review MVO survey results

MVO Funnel: Existing Products

1/3 Build your MVO survey

Before reaching out to your niche for validation, you need to be clear about what, specifically, you are trying to learn.

For existing products, we suggest creating a simple survey for your existing customers to fill out in order to get feedback on an array of different MVOs. By doing so, we can get a sense of which elements within each MVO are most valued by those customers.

We will talk about how to communicate your MVO in the following chapter, but it's important to note that there is some ground work to be done before you send out your survey:

For example, running a workshop with your team & stakeholders to actually generate a few different MVOs. Or, for example, running a batch of user interviews in order to identify specific points of value that you might want to focus on (e.g. being "the fastest" email service).

Once you have a list of 3-8 MVO statements, you can integrate them into the following survey template:

Question 1: What's your full name?

Context: This is so we contact the customer once they have submitted their survey in order to potentially interview them & get more context on their answers

Question 2: Which statement most resonates with you? Select from the list below...

Context: Here you will list all the MVO ideas you have generated in order to see which your customers find most compelling

Question 3: Why did that statement resonate with you?

Context: Here we can gain some insight into why they selected that specific answer

As mentioned previously, Richard, one of our students, used this exact process to re-align his entire company around "fair" compensation for delayed flights.

This clarity - and focus - came from testing out 8 MVOs in a survey sent out to 5,000 of their users, with a few hundred responses providing them with the confidence to reshape their product strategy (and their roadmap) around that specific area of value.

2/3 Get your niche to fill in your MVO survey

In order to get your audience to fill in your MVO survey, it's fairly simple:

Post or reach out directly to them wherever you usually contact them. That might be in a Slack community you run, or sending an email out to your mailing list.

One important consideration, however, is to make sure you are only reaching out to those **in your target audience**.

If, for example, you have decided to focus on a more specific niche of "UX Designers", rather than "tech teams" generally, you do not want to get answers from people who are not UX Designers. This will provide you with inaccurate data - and can easily mislead you.

Remember, the goal is not to get as many survey responses as possible. It is to get **survey responses from the right people**: those within your target niche.

3/3 Review MVO survey results

Once you have got roughly 50-100 responses (enough to give you some confidence in the statistical significance of the survey), you will have a clear idea of which MVOs most resonate with your audience.

Usually, this is fairly clear cut. In Richard's case, for example, there were 3 MVOs that have the vast majority of the votes.

If not clear cut, you may want to iterate your MVOs, or reduce the list of options in the survey, before running it again.

Once you have a clear answer & are happy to commit to your MVO, the next step is to get your team aligned around that MVO.

We'll talk about that more in the next & final chapter:

How to communicate your MVO effectively.

How to Communicate Your MVO?

At this stage, you should have crafted & validated your MVO.

To recap, that means have a clear statement outlining your product strategy that you are confident in committing to, like so:

"We help [niche] achieve [their desired outcome] by [unique way you deliver that outcome]."

Next, you need to learn how to communicate your MVO.

But when it comes to communicating an MVO, what do we really mean?

Communication on a basic level is about how we convey the idea behind the MVO to others in a way that they understand it.

The MVO format itself helps us achieve this; it provides a simple, concrete way to communicate what our product strategy is in a way that others understand (e.g. that "speed" is the most important thing for us to deliver).

As a product leader, however, it is not enough to simply craft & share a great MVO statement.

In order to enact change, however, you must repeatedly communicate the MVO to keep your stakeholders & your team focused on delivering on that MVO.

If you simply craft the MVO, share it with your team, then forget about it, it becomes very easy (and very common) to slowly lose focus, building features that aren't aligned with your product strategy.

The result?

A generic product with lots of unrelated features that don't deliver much value to any specific audience.

This is a certain path to product failure.

How, then, to communicate your MVO in a way that others keep it top of mind? Where it has a constant impact on decision-making when it comes to what we decide to build?

There are many ways we make this happen, such as crafting the product roadmap to align with our product strategy, or giving context around the product strategy before an ideation workshop.

However, unfortunately this is not a book on leadership & communication. This book is about product strategy itself: Understanding what it is & how to define your own product strategy.

We will not go through specific tactics (such as how to run a roadmapping workshop).

Instead, you can use the following guiding principles to determine what makes sense in your specific context in order to not just get people on board with your MVO - but actually keep them on board & keep the MVO top of mind across your product teams.

Principles to help you communicate your MVO:

1. **Repeat. Repeat. Repeat.**
2. **Make your MVO visible**
3. **Make your MVO visual**
4. **Tell stories**
5. **Link every discussion back to your MVO**

1. Repeat. Repeat. Repeat.

Just because a team member says they understand something does not mean they truly have.

This is not the case. In fact, all of us struggle with "the illusion of alignment" where we think we are talking about the same thing when, in fact, we are not.

Take a concept like the "MVP". Everyone has their own interpretation of what this really means. Your CEO might think an MVP is "a rough first version of the eventual product you build. You might, in contrast, think of the MVP as "the most efficient way to generate a key learning". You both use the term MVP, but are, in reality, talking about entirely different concepts.

Furthermore, even when a team member may seem to understand a concept, their thinking might evolve - or they simply forget about it.

Therefore your role is to constantly remind them of exactly what you mean when you try to communicate your MVO. And constantly repeat that key message in every meeting, every interaction, every roadmap item, every retrospective, etc., that you are a part of.

As Jonathan Rosenberg, SVP of Products, Google, wisely states:

> "When you think you've communicated something too much, you're probably just beginning to get through."

So repeat, repeat, repeat. And never stop doing so.

2. Make your MVO visible

Most important strategic work that product teams do is never seen!

It's not good enough to craft an MVO & then leave it in a Google Doc, hidden away in your team's files, quickly forgotten. Instead, you need to make sure your MVO is seen on a daily basis. If you have a physical office, why not have it written out on a white board? If online, why not use our [Miro Product Thinking template](#) as your "home base" to define & communicate key decisions underlying the product strategy.

If your MVO isn't visible, it will be quickly forgotten.

3. Make your MVO visual

Whether you use our [Miro template](#), or any other tool to craft your MVO, the important thing is to visualise the MVO.

Visualisation makes the MVO much more concrete & memorable for your teams.

We strongly suggest using [our Miro template](#) to visualise your MVO.

Firstly, the template clearly highlights the key elements of the MVO to your team (who we are serving, what outcome we should deliver for them, how we will deliver that outcome in a unique way).

Secondly, by highlighting how your product discovery work (those user interviews) flows into the final MVO you decided upon, it's very clear for your existing team - and particularly for new team members - to understand the context behind the decision.

If a new PM, for example, can clearly see the common user frustrations, desired outcomes & how the MVO links these together on a simple Miro board, they are more likely to take ownership & buy-in to the MVO, thus making them more likely to make product decisions aligned with the MVO.

4. Tell stories

> "Stories are 22 times more memorable than facts or figures alone." — Jennifer Aaker, Stanford Graduate School of Business

To reinforce a visual, visible MVO, you can make the MVO even more concrete by telling stories.

The most effective stories will reinforce your MVO. For example, you could talk about different individuals you interviewed & the challenges they faced (e.g. John, who nearly had a nervous breakdown from stress & overwhelm running his first business, QuickFire). Or, to show the impact of your MVO, you could talk about the impact your product has had since you've built solutions aligned with your MVO (e.g. how we've since helped John manage his time & actually enjoy his work!).

Whichever stories you tell, stories are essential to effective communication. As Jonathan Rosenberg, SVP of Products, Google, notes:

> "Narrative is how we learn. If you want to be a leader, you will teach and tell stories. The two are inseparable."

You must therefore go beyond simply showing data or talking through bullet points alone. You must, instead, package your key points into compelling, memorable stories.

5. Link every discussion back to your MVO

Perhaps the easiest on paper, but hardest to follow in practice, it is essential that you take ownership of tying all discussions back to your MVO.

If you have a marketing team, you must ask them:

"Are we effectively communicating our MVO?"

If your team are discussing some cool new feature, you must ask them:

"How does this help us deliver on our MVO? Is it what we believe to be the best way to deliver on our MVO?"

If you are building our roadmap with stakeholders, you must do the same: Ask the team whether this helps us deliver on our MVO.

Whatever the situation, make sure every discussion - and every eventual decision - clearly links back to our MVO (and, by extension, our product strategy).

If not, you shouldn't be considering it.

Whether you prefer workshops to meetings, or you plan your roadmap 12 months ahead rather than just 1 month, follow these principles:

1. **Repeat. Repeat. Repeat.**

2. **Make your MVO visible**
3. **Make your MVO visual**
4. **Tell stories**
5. **Link every discussion back to your MVO**

Internalise them, own them, and adapt them to your unique context. Adapt them to what you believe makes sense, in order to maximise your impact.

Conclusion

Product strategy is **the** foundation for product success.

By being clear about what specific value you deliver with your product - and what value you will *not* deliver - you dramatically increase your chances of success.

Externally, a clear, compelling product strategy makes it infinitely easier to attract, acquire, retain & charge money for your product.

Internally, a clear product strategy becomes "the one decision to solve a thousand decisions".

Decisions around which features to build, previously clouded in confusion, become clear & almost obvious. Rather than constant requests from stakeholders, the product strategy will provide a filter which prevents many irrelevant ideas even coming up in the first place. Rather than struggling to create any value, you'll be laser-focused in creating the *right* value.

Now it's worth being clear:

Product strategy is not the *only* thing that determines success. Factors like how the team executes, team technical capabilities, founder conflict & many other reasons can factor into success or failure.

However, product strategy is a *necessary* part of long-term success. We can survive with founder conflict, for example. We cannot without product strategy. Not in the long-term.

Without product strategy, a product will inevitability lose focus & end up building a generic, low-value product.

What does that mean in practice for you as a product builder?

It means understanding & *applying* everything we have covered. Specifically, those 4 steps:

1. How to **define** the right product strategy to gain initial success
2. How to **validate** your product strategy to know it represents the right thing/s to focus on
3. How to **communicate** that product strategy so people actually follow it
4. Once you've completed Steps 1-3, remaining **relentlessly focused** on executing that product strategy to maintain success

Those steps are not complicated.

Having taught & applied this framework literally hundreds of times, we see many Product Managers & leaders go & apply this framework within their teams with no great difficulty.

In truth:

Product strategy is simple.

We - & many product thought leaders teaching the topic - over-complicate product strategy. Yet that should not stop you from getting started. From experimenting with your own product strategy. From taking all this theory & working out the right product strategy for your team.

The big barrier?

The thing that most prevents action?

You.

You *not* stepping up as a leader - whatever your job title might be - and taking ownership of product strategy.

You *not* being the one who introduces the concept, who works on defining a product strategy, on validating it, on communicating it with your team & stakeholders.

Because it's easy not to.

It's easy to say "not my problem" or "I'm just a Product Manager, so it's not my responsibility". Or to read this book, feel inspired to act, then simply forget to do anything about it.

Yet if you truly want to be a leader & have an impact on your team & on the success of your product, you must make product strategy happen.

Fast-Tracking Your Product Career

Finally, if you are serious about accelerating your product career, check out the next cohort of Prod MBA.

We work with Product Managers & more senior roles to fast-track your path to Head of Product.

How?

We get you to build a real product from zero to revenue over an 8-week, part-time bootcamp. It's the most hands-on, actionable product learning experience out there.

Want to take the next step?

[Check out our next bootcamp here](https://prod.mba) (or visit https://prod.mba)

-

If [Prod MBA](https://prod.mba) is not for you, here are some free resources that can help you keep improving as a product leader:

- [Subscribe to our blog](), where we send out weekly product tips & tactics (prodmba.substack.com)
- [Follow me on LinkedIn](), where I post my thoughts on product & leadership every single day (https://www.linkedin.com/in/henrylatham/)
- [Download the Miro template]() to help you put theory into practice (or see "Product Thinking Board" at https://miro.com/miroverse/profile/prod-mba/)

Printed in Great Britain
by Amazon